Tara's Enlightened Activity

Tara's Enlightened Activity

An Oral Commentary on *The Twenty-one Praises to Tara*

by
Khenchen Palden Sherab Rinpoche
and
Khenpo Tsewang Dongyal Rinpoche

Snow Lion Publications
Ithaca, New York
Boulder, Colorado

SNOW LION PUBLICATIONS
P. O. Box 6483
Ithaca, NY 14851 USA
(607) 273-8519
www.snowlionpub.com

Printed in Canada on acid-free recycled paper.

ISBN-10: 1-55939-287-8
ISBN-13: 978-1-55939-287-7

Tara line drawings by Anna Zhuranskaya, first published in *The Smile of Sun
and Moon* by Khenchen Palden Sherab, translated by Anna Orlova. Boca
Raton, FL: Sky Dancer Press, 2004.

Library of Congress Cataloging-in-Publication Data

Palden Sherab, Khenchen, 1941-
    Tara's enlightened activity : an oral commentary on the twenty-one
praises to Tara / by Khenchen Palden Sherab Rinpoche and Khenpo
Tsewang Dongyal Rinpoche.
        p. cm.
    Includes bibliographical references.
    ISBN-13: 978-1-55939-287-7 (alk. paper)
    ISBN-10: 1-55939-287-8 (alk. paper)
    1. Tara (Goddess)--Prayers and devotions--History and criticism. I. Tsewang
Dongyal, Khenpo, 1950- II. Title.
BQ4710.T33P34 2007
294.3'42114--dc22

                                        2007020381

CONTENTS

PART THREE: DETAILED COMMENTARY ON
THE TWENTY-ONE PRAISES TO TARA

Khenchen Palden Sherab Rinpoche and Khenpo Tsewang Dongyal Rinpoche
with the Tara statue in the Gonpa at Padma Samye Ling

EDITOR'S NOTE

During the more than twenty-five years we have been blessed by their presence in the West, Khenchen Palden Sherab Rinpoche and Khenpo Tsewang Dongyal Rinpoche have given a number of teachings on the Noble Lady Tara. This commentary has been prepared from transcripts of oral teachings given by Khenchen Palden Sherab Rinpoche in Tibetan and translated by Khenpo Tsewang Dongyal Rinpoche. The primary teachings occurred at the Winter Dzogchen Retreat of the Padmasambhava Buddhist Center in January 1997, in West Palm Beach, Florida. Additional details and stories come from Tara teachings given by the Rinpoches in Ellsworth, Maine in May 1992, New York City in March 1996, and Sarasota, Florida in January 2006. Several of the stories about Tara's activities were told during a pilgrimage visit to Nalanda University in India in February 1996. Direction, supplementary materials, and clarifications have been provided through the great generosity of Khenpo Tsewang Dongyal Rinpoche, who has worked patiently with the editor on numerous occasions.

The Tibetan written commentary, composed by Khenchen Palden Sherab Rinpoche during the 1997 retreat and translated into English by Anna Orlova, has already been published as *The Smile of Sun and Moon*.[1] The commentary in the present volume consists of Khenpo Tsewang Dongyal Rinpoche's English translation of the oral teachings. These contain a rich feast of additional explanations and clarifications generously provided from the depths of his devotion and realization of Noble Lady Tara.

The challenge has been to render this oral material, delivered in both formal teaching and conversational formats, into a more structured prose style. We settled on a plan that brings the historical and general commentaries together in the first sections. This arrangement provides the reader with necessary background to then approach the extraordinary, multilayered analysis of the Twenty-one Emanations of Tara which follows.

Most repetitions have been removed. However, students familiar with the Rinpoches will know that there are points to which they return again and again, such as the crucial importance of the bodhichitta motivation. These reminders have been retained as they were given throughout the commentary. We have attempted to preserve the uniquely joyous quality of the Khenpos' humor, their compassion, and their idiomatic references to modern life.

We would like to thank Mimi Bailey, Keith Endo, Ann Helm, Henry Hose, Nancy Roberts, Carl Stuendel, and many others for useful discussions. John Haas and Jane Gilbert very generously peer-reviewed the manuscript. Rita Frizzell of Dakini Graphics provided the design. We also appreciate the assistance of the skilled team at Snow Lion Publications, in particular Steven Rhodes. Any misconceptions or wrong emphases that remain are reflections of the editor's ignorance.

The editor wishes to thank Khenchen Palden Sherab Rinpoche and Khenpo Tsewang Dongyal Rinpoche for the opportunity of deepening my connection and devotion to the Noble Lady Tara in all of her many forms. It is a privilege to be able to offer this small service in bringing their unique and inspired teaching to a wider audience.

May every sentient being experience Tara's blessings!

Pema Drönme (Cynthia Friend)
and the Samye Publishing Group
Padma Samye Ling, May 2007

PART ONE

Noble Lady Tara in
Tibetan Buddhist Life

HISTORY

THE EARLY HISTORY OF TARA PRACTICE

In the course of the third turning of the Wheel of Dharma,[2] Buddha Shakyamuni gave many teachings on Tara within the categories of outer tantra, inner tantra, and the Great Perfection (or *dzogpa chenpo*). All of these, including the Twenty-one Praises to Tara, became very popular in India. They were brought to Tibet in the eighth century at the time of Guru Padmasambhava, King Trisong Deutsen, and master Shantarakshita. Guru Padmasambhava gave many Tara teachings to his heart students, including King Trisong Deutsen and wisdom dakini Yeshe Tsogyal,[3] who was herself an emanation of Tara. Over the next few centuries, Tara became one of the most popular and powerful deities of Tibetan Buddhism.

Within the *Nyingma* or "early translation tradition" of Tibetan Buddhism, Tara practice developed in both *kama* and *terma* lineages. At one time there were three branches of Tara practice within the terma lineage: the large version, the middle version, and the small version. They contain practices on peaceful, semiwrathful, and wrathful emanations of Tara. Though of different lengths and amounts of detail, these practices all had the same nature and the same results. However, each of these three practice lineages became discontinued over time, that is, its transmission, empowerment, and lineage system became disrupted. Even the texts disappeared.

The large version of the Tara practice was revealed in the twelfth century as a terma by a very renowned *tertön* [gter ton] named Guru Tseten. Although he spread the teaching widely and it became very popular, the lineage became interrupted after a few hundred years and disappeared at the level of human practitioners. However, although it seemed to disappear on earth, it continued at the level of the celestial realms and was rediscovered later, as we shall see.

The history of the middle-length Tara practice tells us that it was a terma that Guru Padmasambhava and Yeshe Tsogyal had hidden in Shang Zamphu Lung [shang zam phu lung] in northwest central Tibet. Another famous tertön known as Guru Jobar[4] [gu ru jo 'bar] was intended to be the one to reveal it. The time may not have been right or he may have been caught up in other activities and missed his opportunity. As a result, the text remained hidden for later discovery.

The small version of the Tara practice, also hidden by Guru Padmasambhava and wisdom dakini Yeshe Tsogyal, was revealed by the famous tertön Reshi Lhamo [re kshi lha mo]. He spread the teaching and, though it became very popular for a time, like the large version its lineage became broken.

This does not mean that people ever stopped practicing on Tara! From the time when the Buddha taught on her until today, she has been continually invoked with great devotion. It does mean that the lineages of some of the more profound and secret practices that Guru Padmasambhava initially taught to Yeshe Tsogyal and his other students were interrupted.

Why do difficulties like these arise? The profound Tara teachings are related to the Mother Tantras.[5] These practices are very dear to the wisdom dakinis. Perhaps some of these teachings were not kept well, in the sense that some practitioners did not appropriately honor the wisdom dakinis and Yeshe Tsogyal, and thus the lineages encountered great difficulties. Possibly, because the practices were so unique and secret, the practitioners couldn't handle them correctly at that time.

THE REVIVAL OF TARA PRACTICE IN THE NINETEENTH CENTURY

Early in the nineteenth century, a remarkable group of great masters appeared in the different lineages. They were all close spiritual friends.

At various times each of these masters served as both teacher and student to the others, thus rediscovering, exchanging, and revitalizing the teachings.[6] Their impact was as strong as that of the great masters of early Buddhist history. They brought many lost teachings back to life.

The famous master who is called the Great Khyentse, Jamyang Khyentse Wangpo,[7] held lineages of teachings from all schools of Tibetan Buddhism. Although born into a family of nobility, Khyentse comported himself simply and humbly, carrying his own luggage on pilgrimage. He was both the teacher and student of the first Kongtrül, Jamgön Kongtrül,[8] and was also a root teacher of Mipham Rinpoche.[9] By their time in the nineteenth century, all three categories of Tara practices had already apparently vanished from the human realms, as we described. However, Jamyang Khyentse Wangpo had special powers, or siddhis, and by their use he brought back many of the discontinued teachings. Once, while traveling in central Tibet, the renowned female dharmapala named Tseringma[10] appeared to him, offering all the Tara texts that had disappeared. With her were Guru Padmasambhava, wisdom dakini Yeshe Tsogyal, and the tertön Reshi Lhamo, who gave him empowerment, transmission, and instructions. By powers such as these Jamyang Khyentse Wangpo brought back these and many other lost lineage teachings. He transmitted them to his foremost students, such as the great tertöns Chögyur Dechen Lingpa,[11] Jamgön Kongtrül, and Mipham Rinpoche. All these masters later revealed famous Tara practices at many levels. Their disciples and lineage holders continue to this day.

LINEAGE OF THE PRESENT TEACHINGS ON THE TWENTY-ONE PRAISES TO TARA

This oral commentary is drawn from the teachings of Rongzompa, Taranatha, Jigme Lingpa, and other great masters. Their unbroken lineages merge with the rediscovered termas of Jamyang Khyentse Wangpo, like streams merging into a great river.

Rongzompa[12] was the first recorded source of those of Tara's teachings that are still preserved in Tibet. He was a famous master, great scholar, and highly realized being in the eleventh century. The second master, Taranatha, known as Drölwai Gönpo in Tibetan, was born in 1575.[13] Because of his devotion to Tara, he is generally known by his Sanskrit name, Taranatha, composed of *Tara*, meaning "liberator" and *natha*, or "protector." He was a lineage holder in one of the New Schools, the *Jonangpa*.[14]

Rongzompa's lineage was passed down in the Nyingma School and received by Jigme Lingpa[15] in the eighteenth century. Jigme Lingpa revealed a famous terma on the wisdom dakini Yeshe Tsogyal. Its condensed title is *Dechen Gyalmo*, or "Queen of Great Bliss." He taught that externally we practice on Yeshe Tsogyal as she is, but inwardly we practice on the Twenty-one Emanations of Tara.

For each verse of these Twenty-one Praises to Tara we will present four levels of interpretation: outer or word level; tantra at the Mahayoga and Anuyoga levels; and Dzogchen. They give rise to four different levels of practice on Tara. These are called, respectively, the practice of the Word Meaning, the practice of the General Meaning, the practice of the Hidden Meaning, and the practice of the Ultimate Meaning.

UNDERSTANDING TARA
AT THE RELATIVE LEVEL

Tara is a fully enlightened buddha, who can be understood at both the relative and the ultimate levels.[16] At the relative level, Buddha Tara displays characteristics that can be understood by ordinary, conceptual human minds. Tibetan lore provides an almost limitless supply of wonderful stories about Tara in her relative aspects.

HOW TARA BECAME A BUDDHA

Tara's life story starts by relating how she appeared in the world. One teaching explains how, many eons ago, a princess named Yeshe Dawa, or "Moon of Primordial Wisdom," developed the thought of bodhichitta by the grace of her vast devotion to the buddha of that era. She vowed to become enlightened for the benefit of all the boundless beings who suffered in samsara. The religious leaders of that time, believing that it was only possible to become enlightened in a male body, advised her to pray for a male reincarnation.[17] Princess Yeshe Dawa, however, vowed to attain enlightenment and to carry out all her enlightened activities throughout the three times (past, present, and future) in female form. Eventually this female bodhisattva became a completely enlightened buddha and became known as Tara.

At the ultimate level of wisdom, there is no distinction of male and female. At the relative conceptual level, however, these distinctions are considered to be significant. Each type of physical system, male and female, has its own special strengths in developing our realizations. The female, which is the form that Princess Yeshe Dawa chose, manifests the absolute, open, and spacious nature of mind, which we can call the Great Mother. We will discuss the Great Mother and this openness state in more detail a little later.

Another story of Tara's origins establishes her connection as an emanation of the compassion of Bodhisattva Avalokiteshvara, or Chenrezig. For uncounted eons he had been working tirelessly to fulfill the bodhisattva vow to liberate all sentient beings from suffering. Finally, he felt that his work was completed and that every last being was liberated. He thought that now they were blissfully established in the enlightened state named Potala, the pure land of Avalokiteshvara and Tara.[18] However, when Avalokiteshvara looked again at the six realms,[19] everything was unchanged, still filled with suffering beings! There were just as many, and the same sufferings, miserable conditions, and difficulties were being endured.[20] Seeing that, Avalokiteshvara threw himself on the ground and shed tears of love and compassion. From the tear of his left eye emanated the female bodhisattva White Tara, and from the tear of his right eye emanated Green Tara. Both Taras said, "Don't worry! We two will help you."

TARA'S ENLIGHTENED ACTIVITIES

One of the characteristics of a fully enlightened being is the capacity for enlightened activity. Tara's enlightened activities are numerous and powerful beyond comprehension. For example, at the relative level, she is associated with such beneficial acts as conferring longevity, curing illnesses, stopping wars, and giving prosperity. At the ultimate level she confers all the wisdoms and aspects of realization of ultimate reality. In the following sections of this book, we will learn the specific activities of each of the twenty-one emanations of Tara to whom praise is offered.

Tara is known primarily as "the one who liberates." Especially in the form of the Green Tara, Sengdeng Nagchi Drölma, she liberates sentient beings from the eight great fears.[21] According to Buddha's teaching, these eight great fears can be understood at several levels. For example, one fear is known as the fear of elephants. So, at the outer level, this is the real fear of being harmed by a wild elephant. At the inner level the elephant symbolizes ignorance, so this is the fear of the mental obscuration of ignorance and the sufferings we bring on ourselves and others through acting under the influence of ignorance. We won't go into each of the fears here because the details will be found in the commentary on Sengdeng Nagchi Drölma, the ninth Tara.

Fears that afflict beings exist both externally and inwardly. We can tell by reading the Buddha's teachings that human beings' fears were no different in ancient times than they are in our modern times. Tara's enlightened activity has the potential to protect human beings who connect with her practice from all fears and the causes of these fears.

UNDERSTANDING TARA
AT THE ULTIMATE LEVEL

Tara at the level of absolute truth is beyond understanding based on conceptual thought or analysis. Her true nature is free from mental fabrications, such as the relative concepts of space and time. That which is beyond concepts is difficult both to explain and to understand. Great masters, who have themselves attained realization of the ultimate true nature, have used various images to graciously attempt to describe the indescribable. In speaking of Tara as "the Great Mother" or as "the Wisdom Dakini," the great masters are attempting to guide us towards realization of the nonconceptual Tara.

TARA AS THE ULTIMATE MOTHER

At all levels, from the Hinayana up through the Vajrayana, Buddha Shakyamuni used the language of the Great Mother to explain the ultimate true nature. In fact, at their core, all the teachings of the buddhas are none other than explanations of the nature of the Mother. She is given several different titles, such as Mother of all the Buddhas and Mother of all Samsara and Nirvana.

The ultimate nature is correctly described as our true Mother because she is that which gives birth to and develops our own enlightened mind. For a long time our obscured minds have been distanced from our original nature. Therefore, we wander in samsara lost and confused. Buddha is the one who really points out the way back home and reintroduces us to our own true Mother. If, in that moment, we can jump right into her lap without any fear, we'll reach the highest joy, peace, and realization: the security of the enlightened state.

In the *Prajnaparamita*, or "Perfection of Wisdom," teachings, Buddha taught that, "Those who wish to reach the state of arhats should learn this Mother Prajnaparamita. Those who wish to reach the state of pratyekabuddhas, or solitarily enlightened beings, should learn this Mother Prajnaparamita. Those who wish to reach the state of bodhisattvas, courageous ones with concern for all living beings, should learn this Mother Prajnaparamita. Those who wish to reach the state of buddhas, totally enlightened, free from all obscurations and ego-clinging, fully awakened and heroic, should also realize the Mother nature and practice on the Prajnaparamita." Thus, whatever our level of aspiration and accomplishment, the necessary practice to attain our goal will be the same.

Until now we have been distracted and separated from the recognition of absolute reality, the Mother true nature. Through the Buddha's teachings we are able to learn how to reconnect to our original state, where we will find enjoyment, relaxation, and freedom from confusion. That state is the Mother's beautiful palace or mansion, called the Potala. Her penthouse!

Throughout the sutras and tantras of the Mahayana Prajnaparamita and the Dzogchen, the Buddha taught that we must reconnect ourselves with this Mother. In her ultimate state she is none other than the tathagatagarbha.[22]

THE MOTHER'S INFINITE EMANATIONS

Joy, peace, and enlightenment will come when we reconnect ourselves with our true nature. To provide the opportunity for beings to do this, the Mother herself has emanated in many different sambhogakaya and nirmanakaya forms.[23]

The Mother emanating as nirmanakaya Tara is one of the main deities who deals directly with us confused and distracted beings, and who can bring us back to the original state. Thus Tara is named the mother of both samsara and nirvana. Because her nature is ultimately nondual, Tara's emanations are confined by no boundaries. They go beyond limitations such as geography, tradition, custom, and intellectual or social systems. All of these are dualistic conceptions[24] created by people's mind in relative truth, while Tara resides beyond all such conceptions.

She emanates as needed in her various forms, reaching out to every living sentient being everywhere. Her purpose is to help all living beings, not only selected groups. Thus she aids every type of being, including animals and the beings of other realms, whether or not we can see them.

For human beings Tara emanates in a human form like ours—two arms, two legs, two eyes, and so forth—so her features are familiar. Her traditional costume and adornment, as we see it in thangkas, doesn't look like current West Palm Beach fashion. However, it is very similar to what human beings of the ruling classes wore in ancient India. It's not that she emanated this way because she fancied that particular "look." It was to make it easy for human beings to connect with her so she could bring us to enlightenment. We don't know what Tara's emanations for the other types of beings look like.

Knowing Tara's purpose, we will develop strong feelings of joy, happiness, and closeness at the prospect of connecting to Mother Tara. It is said that Mother Tara's "hook of compassion" is always ready; we must have our mind and heart in the state of readiness, which is the "ring of devotion." We will aspire to follow Tara's example ourselves by working for all living beings with love, compassion, courage, and commitment.

Because Tara abides beyond boundaries and limitations, we cannot exactly say where Tara is and where she is not. Tara is readily available to every living being everywhere. Her sambhogakaya emanations include Vajravarahi, Vajrayogini, the five Mother Dhyani Buddhas, and the five wisdom dakinis. Her nirmanakaya emanations include the Twenty-one Emanations of Tara praised in this homage, plus many more in all the different colors. Red Tara, for example, is special for activating our realization and overpowering our ego-clinging and neurotic states. With her help we are freed from the confinement of our egos so we are able to reach out to all living beings with bodhichitta.

In India Tara's famous emanations include wisdom dakinis Mandarava and Niguma and in Tibet, wisdom dakinis Yeshe Tsogyal and Machig Labdron. Tara has so many emanations we cannot begin to grasp them with the conceptual mind. Not all of Tara's emanations have been widely recognized or renowned; some are very humble, anonymous persons, and others are not so much persons as very subtle energies.[25]

Among all these emanations, it is sufficient for us to practice just one. Green Tara, White Tara, Red Tara, Yeshe Tsogyal, or Vajrasarasvati practice can remove our fears, obscurations, and obstacles, help us develop the ability to benefit all beings, and assist us to reach enlightenment. Yet Buddhism, especially in its Vajrayana form, is new in the Western countries. For Western students who have strong interest, devotion, and dedication, it is a source of inspiration to be introduced to all the powerful and profound levels of meaning of Tara, the Great Mother and wisdom dakini.

The specific practice we are discussing is called the Twenty-one Praises to Tara.[26] Here we see twenty-one different Taras, with different names, colors, and so forth. You might well ask why there are twenty-one Taras. Why not twenty-three, or thirty, or forty, or just ten? The number twenty-one has specific symbolic meanings. At the basic level,[27] the Buddha taught twenty-one techniques with which we may work to attain enlightenment.

According to the Mahayana sutra system, as we practice we traverse the ten different levels, or bhumis,[28] eventually reaching the enlightened state. The basis for our enlightenment is right where we find ourselves now, with the precious endowment of our own human body and our own buddha-nature.

Vajrayana, or tantra, is similar to the sutra system, but its methods are more specifically targeted. According to tantric teaching, within this human body we have twenty-one different knots. These are in pairs and they obstruct or block our channels. Through practice, as we release each of these pairs of knots, we obtain a specific experience or realization. After we have released all of the twenty-one knots, we are known as enlightened beings, having attained buddhahood.

Of course, buddhahood is not some force that is outside us, waiting for the knots to be untied in order to come in! From basic Buddhism all the way to Dzogchen, it is made perfectly clear that buddhahood is an innate state, already within us. Our inherently awakened state is an already enlightened being, a buddha, the tathagatagarbha. When we release those twenty-one knots, we attain the ultimate awakening known as the dharmakaya state.

The dharmakaya, in turn, has twenty-one spontaneously inherent qualities.[29] They transcend duality, the compounded state, permanence and impermanence, and effort or striving. Unceasingly they arise as necessary for the benefit of all sentient beings. These twenty-one active dharmakaya qualities appear as the twenty-one emanations of Tara. Thus Tara combines all the active energies of the three kayas by which we release our own knots and those of other beings, the energy by which we achieve enlightenment and help other beings to achieve it.

TARA AND THE WISDOM DAKINI

As the embodiment of enlightened energy, Tara is inseparable from the wisdom dakini. Guru Padmasambhava's retinue certainly included some dakas, but many more were dakinis. The Sanskrit terms *daka* and *dakini* translate into Tibetan as *khandro* and *khandroma*. In English we might say "sky-walker" or "sky-goer." Or maybe UFO! There are many beautiful teachings about the deeper meanings of these terms. "Sky" refers to wisdom, and "goer" refers to love and compassion, which are the wisdom dakini's beneficial activities. An expanded meaning of dakini would be "the activity of love and compassion, full of strength, moving freely in the wisdom space."

There are many different types of dakinis, such as earthly dakinis, action dakinis, and wisdom dakinis. Dakinis are usually pictured as beautiful, young, and dancing in the sky, but some, such as the Lion-Headed Dakini[30] and Black Tröma,[31] are frightening in appearance. Wisdom dakinis Mandarava and Yeshe Tsogyal were famous both as Guru Rinpoche's students and also as great teachers, helping to preserve the teachings as termas for future times.[32] These wisdom dakinis are a little like the Western "Superwoman" or other superheroines.

As we turn our attention to the wisdom dakini nature of Tara, this will bring us into a consideration of the deep meaning of the true nature of our minds and of reality. When we begin to study and practice and we start looking beyond externals to internal levels, we know intellectually there will be much to discover. Initially we can't penetrate deeper levels very well because our present consciousness and senses are deluded by habitual patterns of conceptual and dualistic thinking. No matter how carefully and openly we try to look and think about things, our view is always partial, limited. That's just how our mental habits have developed. Of course, what we're able to see now, limited though it is, seems to fulfill our everyday needs so we don't think there's anything wrong with it!

But then, inspired by the teachings, we do try to look deeper. At first we find we're unable to perceive any reality beyond our habitual pattern, even though we have adequate eyes, ears, nose, tongue, body, and mental capacities. The perceptions of our six senses are trapped by our old attitudes of partiality and limitation. We're always setting up rules and mental boundaries. Once we start to take note, we'll see that we entrap ourselves in every direction with a web of concepts. Skillful and determined practice is needed in order to break the pattern and see beyond. Once that happens, our wisdom mind sees the true nature of reality as vastness from which arises an unceasing display of dynamic forms called the display of the mandala of the wisdom dakinis.

That's why the great masters teach about developing the openness state symbolized by the dakini's third eye.[33] Her third eye, or wisdom mind, sees beyond duality. For the wisdom mind there are no boundaries or limitations. For example, an individual with the realization of the wisdom mind makes no distinction between past, present, and future. All are seen in one instant.

Our wisdom must be developed inwardly; it has nothing to do with external conditions. Our dualistic minds have also developed inwardly; we are internally obscured. The mind's true nature is always buddha-nature and its experience is perfect joy and peace. Everything feels really smooth and perfect in the enlightened state with no bumpy situations at all!

This understanding will develop according to our stage of realization. To the extent that we cleanse our minds of habitual patterns, we become more able to see the clear image of absolute truth. For example, when we are recovering from hepatitis, as the jaundice clears from our eyes and our vision clears up, we begin to see a brighter external reality. Similarly, as we gradually clear out our internal habitual patterns, our understanding becomes clear.

Realizations come only if we practice joyfully, with confidence and courage. Realization doesn't grow within a timid or weak state of mind—it blossoms in the mind free of doubt and hesitation. Realization is fearless. When we see the true nature of reality, there's nothing hidden, nothing left to fear. At last we're seeing reality as it is, full of joy and peace.

Our habitual patterns can only be removed by understanding the great emptiness aspect of true nature, that which is named the Mother of all the buddhas. Emptiness is freedom; emptiness is great opportunity. It is pervasive and all phenomena arise from it. As the great master Jigme Lingpa said, "The entire universe is the mandala of the dakini." The Mother's mandala is all phenomena, the display of the wisdom dakini.

Without this ultimate great emptiness, the Mother of the buddhas, the universe would be without movement, development, or change. Because of this great emptiness state of the Mother, we see phenomena continually arising. Each display arises, transforms, and radiates, fulfilling its purpose and then dissolving back into its original state. This dramatic dance of energy is the activity, ability, or mandala of the wisdom dakini. Thus, the combination of the great emptiness or openness state, together with the activities of love and compassion, is both the ultimate Mother and the ultimate wisdom dakini.

This ultimate nature of reality is not separate from the nature of the mind. We should not disconnect them. When we look into our own mind, we see that it's also based on this great emptiness wisdom state. We won't find anything substantially existing because this Mother is beyond conceptions and habit patterns. Yet our thoughts and conceptions, which are mental phenomena, continually arise from the mind's true nature, each thought fulfilling its own purpose, then dissolving back into the original state. There are no solid entities at all, just an unceasing display of dynamic form; as it is called for, it appears. That is how mind is the display of the mandala of the wisdom dakinis.

Try not to spoil this arising energy of love and compassion of the wisdom dakini with ego-clinging. Ego is duality; ego-clinging or grasping is an obscuration that disturbs the radiating energy of the wisdom dakini. It also disturbs our practice, so we must try to release it, or at least ease it, by developing more love, compassion, and openness. This is the essence of Dzogchen and of the Buddhadharma.

DEEPENING OUR UNDERSTANDING OF EMPTINESS

What is emptiness? We have said it is a state full of freedom and opportunity. It is the pervasive nature of every external and internal sense object and the source of every outer and inner display. As the *Heart Sutra* says, "Emptiness is form; form is emptiness. Emptiness is none other than form; form is none other than emptiness." Furthermore, emptiness is the source of our minds. Mind resides totally within this great emptiness state. Try as we might, we cannot grasp our own mind. That is as useless as grasping at the sky.

It is easy to misunderstand this English word "emptiness" as implying blankness, or vacancy, or an astronomer's "black hole." The Tibetan word for this, *tong pa nyi* [stong pa nyid], does not suggest such inappropriate meanings. It is also possible to misconstrue emptiness as a state of destruction or a space left where something has been destroyed. To avoid this error Madhyamaka philosophers taught the example of a big clay pot sitting on a table. Imagine that suddenly someone comes by and hits it with a hammer and crack! That clay pot is gone. What has happened to the pot? What happened to the pot is not emptiness. So when we hear the Buddha's teachings on emptiness, we shouldn't think of something like a smashed clay pot.

When the *Heart Sutra* says, "Emptiness is form; form is emptiness," we could compare emptiness to a rainbow. When we see a glorious rainbow in the sky, we see clearly all its beautiful colors, but yet we cannot grasp or touch it—we'd just get wet. We can't keep it—it will vanish soon no matter what we do. We can even pass right through a rainbow—there is nothing solidly existing about it. A rainbow, then, makes a really good metaphor for this great emptiness. The room, the temple, or whatever location we are at right now is no different than a rainbow. We, ourselves, are none other than a rainbow. This is a true understanding of the great emptiness.

There is nothing solidly existing anywhere. If we attempt to grasp or cling to people, places, or possessions, we're trying to grab a rainbow. We are trying to reprogram the original state of the true nature. Such efforts are futile! From our futile grasping arise hope, fear, and all our different emotions and experiences.

All the great masters tell us, "Go beyond dualities; relax; don't hope; don't grasp; let it go. Flow continually in the relaxing original state." Because the true nature is nonduality, when we connect our minds to the flowing system of the true nature, then joy, peace, love, and compassion naturally arise without any effort. Love, compassion, courage, and commitment are qualities of the true nature of our own minds. Only our dualistic habit patterns prevent these noble qualities from radiating. As we begin to break through these habitual patterns, the energy of our true nature begins to shine effortlessly to help all sentient beings. Duality changes to nonduality and there is no more burden or pressure.

How are buddhas really able to see every single being?[34] How are the buddhas' love and compassion really able to encompass them all? Buddha Shakyamuni said, "When you have the realization of the true nature of reality and the nature of your own mind, then you will see the whole world differently. The pure land is right here—it's not really far away." H.H. Düdjom Rinpoche said, "If you would like to see pure lands, purify your conceptions and the beautiful pure land is right in front of you." He means that when realization comes, we will become able to see the many beautiful things in this universe that we had been unable to see. We will become able to see the many different beings whom we had been unable to see with our obscured vision, such as the emanations of the daka and dakini. We will also be able to perform enlightened activities. All the ancient great masters, with the realization or understanding of their true natures, experienced these results and so will we.

PART TWO

*An Approach to the
Tantric Practice of Tara*

A BRIEF DESCRIPTION
OF TANTRA

When we practice the Twenty-one Praises to Tara, the actual words of the translation constitute the outer meaning. However, there are several additional levels of meaning we may explore, each pointing us to another level of our inner realization. Therefore, we will teach each Praise at four levels: its outer meaning, two aspects of its tantric meaning, and its meaning according to the Dzogchen view.

What is the word meaning of "tantra"?[35] *Tantra* is a Sanskrit word, which translates into Tibetan as *rgyud*, pronounced *gyü*. This in turn translates into English as "continuity, continuum."

TANTRA'S THREE ASPECTS OF GROUND, PATH, AND FRUIT

The three aspects of tantra are known as the ground (*zhi*), path (*lam*), and fruit (*dre bu*). We may regard them as, respectively, the foundation (or base) of tantra; the application of tantra; and the achievement (or result) of tantra.

The Ground (or Base Level) of Tantra

What is this ground, or base, of tantra? The ground of tantra is simply the true nature of our own mind, buddha-nature, also known as tathagatagarbha. In tantric terms this foundation is known as the "youthful vase body."[36] No one's basic nature is old or ready to retire! It is vigorous and healthy. This youthful state is not something we're currently working on developing or that we acquired last year. From beginningless time until now, it continues uninterrupted and unceasing. Thus the base of tantra is this continuum, our original, authentic nature. Of course, none of this is too obvious to us at the moment, while our true nature is still obscured by our habits of duality. We must practice intelligently and intensively in order to reveal this ground.

The Path (or Application Level) of Tantra

To reveal our original nature we turn to the second aspect of tantra: the path, or application. Just as the base is continuous, we must apply our practice without interruption. We carry on until our original nature is fully revealed.

How should we apply ourselves? The Buddha taught that we should reveal our true nature by applying both method and wisdom. Method equals skillful means, primarily love and compassion. Wisdom is having a mind free from attachment or grasping. Continually developing and uniting love and compassion with nonattachment, we reveal the ongoing youthful vase body, or the continuum of our basic nature.

In the Vajrayana approach to attaining realization, one uses creation stage practice and completion stage practice. Creation stage, or visualization, practice is a skillful means practice to develop love and compassion. Completion stage, or dissolving, practice, on the other hand, is direct practice on nongrasping; it is a wisdom practice in which we pass beyond relying on our conceptual imagination. Thus, creation and completion stage practices are the same as practicing skillful means and wisdom.

Skillful means and wisdom, practiced with courage, commitment, and joy, will transform all emotional obscurations and habitual patterns into the mind's original state. Our habitual patterns cease to be habitual, our grasping becomes nongrasping, and our clinging becomes nonclinging. Then these are no longer obstacles for us. In fact, these phenomena become assistants to the growth of our realization, helping us to radiate love and compassion in every direction. At that point, we've actualized our own nature as the youthful vase body, the ground (or base) of tantra, which has no characteristics, no labels or dualities. What we've discovered is what we always really had. It's nothing newly arisen, but just what was inherent. What we've discovered is the true face of the ultimate Mother. The ancient masters often use a metaphor of the "meeting of the mother and child" for this wonderful rediscovery. And, as we've said before, Tara is none other than this ultimate Mother whom we meet.

The Fruit (or Achievement Level) of Tantra

In Dzogchen teaching, the stage of realization called "meeting of the mother and child" is the peak. The Great Mother is named Samantabhadri. Samantabhadri is a Sanskrit name that translates into Tibetan as *Kuntuzangmo*. In English it means "always good, perfect." So she is known as the Always-Good Mother. This Mother will never scold you! The discovery of our nature as the perfection of Kuntuzangmo's nature is the fruit, or achievement aspect, of tantra. Don't be misled by the word "achievement." This is not some new award or prize to "get." The fruit is inherent—it is a continuity and we simply rediscover it.

To summarize, even though our original nature (the ground) has been here all along, we couldn't connect with it before due to our heavy habits of duality. But by practicing skillful means and wisdom (the path), we have discovered the original youthful vase body, the continuing nature state of tantra, and attained the fruition which was inherently ours all along, realization or buddhahood.

THE SIX LIMITS AND THE FOUR SYSTEMS

Each of Buddha's tantric teachings is very profound, having multiple levels on which to examine truths and many ways to reveal the true nature of the mind. The goal is always to bring ourselves and all living beings to enlightenment and to bring joy and peace.

A tantra may thus have meanings on many levels. Some meanings will be accessible to ordinary beings living in a particular time and place; other meanings are only understandable to beings that are at stages farther along the path to enlightenment. In fact, some meanings are only to be understood and applied by bodhisattvas or buddhas who have reached enlightenment and are actively bringing everyone to the enlightened state. If we only rely on our ordinary point of view when trying to make sense of tantra, some misunderstanding could occur. Therefore, receiving the pith instructions directly from a qualified lineage holder is the key to opening the total meaning of the teaching.

Then to unlock this essential meaning of the tantra, the pith instructions, we must follow a series of methods. These are known as the six limits and the four systems, or meanings. These ten approaches taken all together will bring out the perfect, accurate meaning of the tantra. The six limits are pervasive. They apply to how we understand the text as a whole. However, we apply the four systems directly to the interpretation of each word and line.

The Six Limits

In Tibetan, the six limits are *tha drug*. Consider these six limits as six different keys for unlocking the subtle tantric words of Buddha so we may correctly understand their deeper meaning. There are three pairs of alternatives. The first and second limits relate to whether a teaching's meaning is found at the mundane level or at the nonmundane level. Sometimes the Buddha gave simple teachings that were intended for that time and place, for the time being. Such teachings have indirect, or relative, meanings designed to connect with the minds of ordinary beings and redirect them toward the path of enlightenment. At those times the Buddha chose not to challenge everyone's strong grasping at duality. Instead, he would calmly and skillfully accept the notions that deluded beings held and teach them with mundane meanings. This is known as *drang dön yin pa*, meaning for the mundane level. At a more advanced stage, such as in the *Heart Sutra*, he would lead them into more profound states. This nonmundane aspect of the teaching is *drang dön ma yin pa*. It can also be called the certain meaning, or *nges dön*.

The third and fourth limits relate to whether the meaning is explicit or hidden. If Buddha was giving a teaching with both ordinary words and hidden meanings, it is called *gong pa chen*. The hidden meanings correspond to the absolute truth. If his purpose was to explicitly explore relative truth, without hidden meanings, it is called *gong pa chen min pa*.

The fifth and sixth limits describe whether the word meaning is to be taken literally or understood symbolically. If it can be taken literally, it is *dra gi zhin chen yin pa*. On the other hand, if it makes no apparent sense to us, it is a clue that this teaching is symbolic, or *dra gi zhin chen ma yin pa*.[37] Since tantric teachings often have complex symbolic meanings behind them, if we go along just with what a text seems to say on the surface, there may be a serious misunderstanding. Therefore, as many great masters said, when we begin to study the Buddha's tantric teachings directly, we must have the keys.

Where do we find the keys with which to study and practice tantra? Please remember that while we can learn a great deal from books, we must have the instructions of a qualified lineage master to practice tantra. He or she holds the keys to unlock these special teachings originally sealed by the Buddha.

The Four Systems of Meaning

The four modes are the *tshül zhi*. *Zhi* is "four," and *tshül* is "systems," "modes," or "aspects." The first mode is the word meaning: *tshig gi tshül*; second is the general meaning: *chi'i tshül*; third is the hidden meaning: *be dön gyi tshül*; and fourth is the ultimate meaning: *thar thug gi tshül*. From each of these modes of meaning emerges a particular approach to meditation and practice. Thus, we will apply each of these four to each of the Twenty-one Praises to Tara. In this way we will reveal and display the full depth of meaning of what these great masters taught. The four corresponding practice systems will be described in the next section.

THE FIVE PERFECTIONS
OF THE TEACHING

The great Indian masters always presented the Buddha's teachings with a description of the Five Perfections. Whenever Buddha gave a teaching, the beneficial causes and conditions of these Five Perfections were always present. Thus Buddha's wisdom energy was able to radiate in all directions to awaken everyone into the enlightened state.

The Five Perfections are:
- the perfect teacher
- the perfect students
- the perfect place
- the perfect occasion
- the perfect content

First, who taught this teaching? It was taught by the perfect teacher, the Buddha Shakyamuni. In many of the Tara tantras, the concluding section states that it was taught by the Buddha Vairochana. Symbolically, this tells us that the Buddha Shakyamuni appeared in the form of the Buddha Vairochana in order to give these Vajrayana teachings.

Who is Buddha Vairochana? According to Dzogchen, Buddha Vairochana is an emanation of the Buddha Samantabhadra[38] and is one of the five Dhyani Buddhas.[39] Each of the five is connected with a different element, aggregate, color, and mental obscuration. Each exemplifies a specific aspect of primordial wisdom. These five wisdoms represent the union of love, compassion, and wisdom, as discussed earlier, inherent within the nature of our minds and none other than the youthful vase body.

Vairochana represents solidity, the center or foundation, as he is associated with the earth element and the form aggregate, the basis of the other aggregates. Among the five wisdoms, he is connected with the dharmadhatu wisdom.[40]

Because he realized perfectly the nature of the five wisdoms, Buddha Shakyamuni is the embodiment of the five Dhyani Buddhas. In his perfectly enlightened state, he began to radiate the energy of the Buddha Vairochana and to give these Tara teachings. Thus the Buddha Shakyamuni is the perfect teacher.

Now, to whom did he teach? His retinue were the perfect students. When Buddha gave these Tara teachings, all the great arhats and bodhisattvas were there, as well as the four other Dhyani Buddhas. All these beings were highly enlightened, beyond duality and conceptions, so they are known as the perfect retinue.

Where were the teachings given? They were given in the pure land of Akanishtha,[41] a Sanskrit name for the pervasive land which is beyond size and measure. Akanishtha is known as the perfect place. It is beyond duality and cannot be understood by dualistic thoughts.

When did Buddha give these teachings? We cannot apply dualistic frameworks, such as time or place, to perfect teachings. At the ultimate level, conceptual limitations such as time are irrelevant. The Vajrayana is a timeless, uninterrupted teaching. This is yet another way in which the word "tantra," or gyü, means "continuity." The Buddha is giving these teachings now, beyond duality, in Akanishtha, the land without measure. The perfect time is the time beyond the three times of conceptual minds—original time. The teaching exists in an ongoing effortless state, echoing energy.

What did the Buddha teach? A perfect teaching is one which is taught with perfected skillful means and wisdom.[42] Since the Tara tantras are teachings on skillful means and wisdom, they are perfect teachings. This Tara teaching was given to beings of all levels of capacity by teaching on all levels of tantra, from the Kriyatantra through the inner tantras. Our teaching, too, will encompass all levels of tantra, including the Dzogchen understanding.

How to Practice Tara

In the simplest terms, what do we mean when we talk about practicing on Tara? We mean: connecting our minds and hearts to Mother Tara and following the model of Mother Tara's fearless and compassionate behavior.

How to Set up a Shrine to Tara

The shrine is a reminder of our practice and meditation, so it is known as a support of the practice. It reminds us of what we would like to actualize. Before we sit we do three prostrations. Why do we prostrate? Prostrations are an expression of our deep reverence and appreciation for the practice. What is it that we are intending to practice? We're not just practicing increased ego-clinging or control. We're not thinking of personal rewards or of impressing others. These would not deserve respect! Truly we're practicing Tara's true love, compassion, wisdom, and nonviolence. Tara's love and compassion have no discrimination and are total peace and happiness. Thus we joyfully do three prostrations to the shrine, which symbolizes our practice, with profound reverence deep down in our heart. We chant, "Namo Buddhaya; Namo Dharmaya; Namah Sanghaya."

If the situation doesn't allow all this, then simply practice. The shrine, shrine objects, and prostrations are just symbols and symbols are not necessary for practice. Our meditation, practice, confidence, commitment, and bodhichitta are the true shrine, which is in our hearts. They are the objects of veneration. Do not let these precious qualities fall down on the ground, but always honor and respect them. They will grow everlastingly and glorify the dignity of our nature.

Our Tara practice may develop at any of the four levels, from very simple to very elaborate. Different types of shrines are appropriate for each level. At the simpler levels, we prepare a small shrine in a quiet, pleasant spot, with a picture or statue of Tara. Green Tara's picture is perhaps best, as she is really the source of all the Taras. In front of her image, place offerings of incense, a flower, and a lamp or candle. In everyone's eyes flowers are beautiful, so at least offer flowers to honor your practice and your meditation.

For a more complex practice, we can assemble a shrine of two or three levels. The first level is square and roughly the height of an arrow, covered with a red cloth. The second level is placed upon the first. It is a platform a few inches high with a surface smaller than the lower one and also covered with red cloth. The top level is still smaller. On this third platform there should be three images: a statue or image of Buddha Shakyamuni in the center and images of Guru Padmasambhava on his right and of Tara on his left.

On the first level, either place a paper drawing of Tara's mandala or arrange on a plate five small heaps of rice in the four directions and center. Centered on the first level there should also be a *bumpa*, or ritual vase, with a sprinkler of peacock feathers to which is attached a picture of Tara. The spout of the bumpa, the peacock feathers, and Tara's picture should all face us as we sit in front of the shrine. Prepare saffron water, with other blessing substances if available, to put in the vase.

For offerings, if available, place tormas and small metal skull cups filled with blessing substances on the shrine. If we don't have them, it is all right too.

For an even more elaborate inner tantra practice, we may construct an additional offering. Place a tripod in the center of the shrine and upon it a skull cup with its narrower end facing forward. In the skull cup place melted butter containing blessing materials of the lineage. When the butter is solid, write the Tibetan letter BAM on its surface, then add either an alcoholic beverage or pure spring water layered over the butter. Place a triangle made of wooden pieces on top of the tripod with one point facing front. It is covered with a red cloth folded into four layers, and on the cloth is placed a ritual mirror, or *melong*, coated with red dust in which the syllable TAM is written. On top of all these, place a quartz crystal.

But if we don't have all these objects and cannot do this sort of thing, it is really all right. Tibetans have always practiced Tara spontaneously, freely, and easily, reciting her mantra while cooking food, planting crops, or in any ordinary place and time. Since Tara is none other than our own true nature, she's always there.

SPECIAL TIMES AND PLACES TO PRACTICE

The teachings recommend particular times and places to practice for powerful results. The many secret holy places in the world include the Earth's twenty-four power spots or acupuncture spots, thirty-two holy places, and eight great cemeteries. Guru Padmasambhava said that dakas and dakinis gather to perform ceremonies at those places at specific times such as the tenth and twenty-fifth days of the lunar month.[43] The twenty-fifth day is when practices of the female deities, such as Tara, and the dakini practices are most effective. If we perform practice on those special days it will help to release the knots of our channels and bring a clear understanding, or instant realization, of the wisdom energy nature of our minds and our bodies. If we practice with the right intention, without grasping and clinging, then realizations will emanate and radiate.

MANTRA RECITATION

Mantra is a profound way to practice Mother Tara. We can't put a picture or statue of Mother Tara inside us, but we can generate the sacred sound energy of Tara inside us. Sound is powerful; it's a gateway or bridge between the world of form and the formless. Mantra is sacred sound. It didn't originate with some ordinary person or thing, but it is the self-voice or original sound of the natural state. Furthermore, the mantra is not just something we are "putting out," it's also something that we are taking in to help ourselves self-actualize. When we first begin to say mantra, we should simply try to be aware that the mantra is more than just our own voice making a series of noises. Realize that the mantra is alive, a manifestation of our inner vajra nature.

Tara's mantra of ten syllables is:

ༀ་ཏུ་རེ་ཏུཏྟ་རེ་ཏུ་རེ་སྭ་ཧཱ།

OM TARE TUTTARE TURE SOHA

We may use this mantra for practicing on all of Tara's emanations.[44] The first syllable OM invokes auspiciousness, peace, and balance. OM is also connected to the body of the buddhas. It grounds us in the practice. TARE, just like *Drölma*, Tara's Tibetan name, refers to her as the swift and heroic liberator. When you're a hero, you love what you're doing. So Tara is enthusiastic! TARE liberates us from fears and troubles; more profoundly, she liberates us from samsara. TUTTARE reflects her powerful activity of fulfilling all wishes; more profoundly, she brings us to nirvana. With TURE, we move beyond both samsara and nirvana to the ultimate nondual state of the dharmakaya. Finally, SOHA establishes us in the state of complete enlightenment, "firmly like a driven stake."

There are many instructions on how to say mantra. We have heard many great masters chant and each did it a little differently. But in general, we think that mantra should be chanted "like the sound of bees nesting," just loudly enough so we can be sure we're pronouncing each syllable. Chant mantra continuously, without a definite beginning and end to each repetition. Chant with a speed that is as quick as possible while allowing you to keep each syllable clearly in mind. Each syllable is equally important. Meditate that the inner sound of the true nature is merging with the voice.

Mantra recitation is usually combined with a visualization in which we see the mantra circling in the deity's heart-center and experience its sound as self-reciting. Nevertheless, if we can't do this visualization process too clearly, we should not feel guilty or discouraged at our limited capabilities. After all, sentient beings all have limitations. In every aspect of our practice, we should be happy with what we are able to do today and aspire to be able to do more tomorrow. Remember that Tara won't mind. Just don't forget her! That is the key.

A SOUND FRAMEWORK FOR A COMPLETE PRACTICE

Three fundamental qualities must be present for any practice to be as beneficial as possible for us and other beings. These qualities are called the *dam pa sum*, or "three supreme practices."[45] Without them, our practice will be, at best, incomplete. At worst, misdirected effort may possibly even strengthen our ego-clinging and negativity of mind.

The Supreme Preparation: Developing Bodhichitta

The first supreme quality describes the quality of preparation with which we begin our practice. The best preparation we could possibly have is to successfully develop the supreme motivation, which is bodhichitta. Thus, before we start any dharma practice, we should develop this quality with intensity, "from the core of our hearts and the marrow of our bones." We should develop powerful feelings of love and compassion for all beings, freshness and interest in the practices we are about to do, and closeness to the enlightened beings whose practice we are about to begin. We should then meditate with courage and commitment on the four immeasurables, or four boundless ones. These are: boundless love, boundless compassion, boundless joy, and boundless equanimity.[46]

With that preparation every teaching becomes a great source of wisdom and a great inspiration. We also never become bored and tired of our practice. Sometimes when we don't develop the first supreme one regularly and intensely enough, we may start with enthusiasm, but then our practice collapses. On the other hand, if we repeatedly, firmly reestablish our feelings of love, compassion, joyfulness in effort, and freshness, our practice will become an undying practice, continually staying in a state of growth. So motivation is really important!

Clearly recognize that this is the precious ground where every beautiful thing grows and develops. Whether receiving teachings, contemplating teachings, meditating on teachings, doing formal practice, or carrying out positive activities, combine all of this with bodhichitta and the four immeasurables. Bring whatever arises into the practice and transform it into joy, peace, and benefit for others and ourselves.

The Supreme Attitude during Practice: Nongrasping

The second supreme quality describes the attitude with which we carry out the main part of the practice. Whether we practice according to the general, hidden, or ultimate meaning, we must practice in a nonconceptual way. Not too much grasping and clinging! Let it come, let it go; open the heart as well as the eyes, bright as sunshine. Then carry out the activities of meditating, visualizing, reciting mantra, or just being absorbed totally in the Dzogchen meditation state.

The Supreme Conclusion: Dedication of the Merit

The third supreme quality describes how we should conclude the practice with the powerful activity of dedicating the merit of our practice. We offer generous aspirations, good wishes, and a good heart for all living beings. We always include ourselves to honor our own precious human existence.

If we begin our practice with bodhichitta motivation, carry it out with a nongrasping attitude, and conclude it with dedications, aspirations, and a good heart, every practice is a perfect practice. If we place it within this threefold framework, the simplest practice can become the most powerful practice imaginable in its benefits to us and all beings.

WORKING WITH THE FOUR LEVELS OF PRACTICE

As mentioned before, the teachings and practice of tantra are traditionally given according to four levels: outer, inner, secret, and very secret. According to our capabilities and following the instructions of our teachers, we may practice on Tara at any or all of these four. What follows is a brief general description of each of the four levels.

The Practice of the Word Meaning

The simplest approach to Tara's practice is that of the word meaning, or outer meaning. At this simple level we may read the words and think about them, look at the beautiful drawings, and perhaps memorize and recite the words of the Twenty-one Praises to Tara, in Tibetan or English, as we prefer.

These Praises originated in India as a Sanskrit prayer. In the eighth century Guru Padmasambhava, King Trisong Deutsen, and the great master Shantarakshita had it translated from Sanskrit into Tibetan. Many great masters from India and Tibet worked together, carefully discussing how to translate each word. The Indian and Tibetan scholars developed a unified translation system, with a standardized list of translation equivalents.

Because Tara has now become a very popular deity in the West, several masters with their students have translated the Twenty-one Praises into Western languages. At the moment there are more than a dozen variations on the English word meaning in print. However, here in the West, while everyone has done their best in trying to convey the meaning, there's no consistency among these modern translations. We will use the word (or outer) meaning of each verse of the Twenty-one Praises to Tara according to the English translation by Anna Orlova, which was prepared under our direction.[47]

The Sanskrit and Tibetan languages, more so than English, encourage and value a style of poetry in which a word or phrase may have two to four layers of meaning. Thus, no simple word translation can begin to capture all the profound meanings of these beautiful poems. Furthermore, as the Twenty-one Praises to Tara is a tantric teaching with symbolic meanings, we will be carefully analyzing the words used according to the system of the six limits, as previously described.

The Practice of the General Meaning

In the general (or inner) meaning, we practice with a visualization, so it is development (or generation stage) practice, or *kye rim* [bskyed rim]. In Vajrayana there are different techniques for visualization. Simply, we may either visualize the deity in front of ourselves or we may self-visualize or self-generate ourselves as the deity. In practicing the Twenty-one Praises to Tara, we visualize each Tara individually and sequentially in two stages or steps. We start by visualizing Tara right in front of us. Once this front visualization of Tara becomes stable, then we can visualize her dissolving into us, and we become as Tara.

The general appearance of each Tara is the same. She has one face, two arms, and two legs. Her left hand displays the protection mudra,[48] which stops difficulties and misery, while holding the stem of an utpala, or blue lotus flower. The open bloom is next to her left shoulder and on its upturned surface rests a symbolic object. Her right hand is held downward in the supreme bestowing mudra.[49] She sits upon a lotus and moon disc with her left leg bent and her right leg partially extended in the dismounting posture, or posture of royal ease. The individual details of the visualization, such as the color of each Tara's body, the expression of her face, and the symbolic object upon her lotus blossom, will be specified in the sections to come. From Tara and the symbolic object she holds, various sounds and lights emanate. In each case we visualize these as carrying out specific wisdom activities.

While maintaining this visualization, we recite Tara's mantra of ten syllables:

ཨོཾ་ཏཱ་རེ་ཏུཏྟཱ་རེ་ཏུ་རེ་སྭཱ་ཧཱ།

OM TARE TUTTARE TURE SOHA

Recite the mantra with clarity and concentration as much as possible. Here, mantra recitation is the essential point.

The Practice of the Hidden Meaning

The hidden (or secret) meanings of each of the praises to Tara contain instructions on working with the yogas of the body's channels, winds, and essences. These are referred to as the "completion stage practices with concepts," *dzog rim* [rdzogs rim]. Historically speaking, all Vajrayana teachings were considered secret, from the Kriyatantra through the Dzogchen. These teachings were not in line with the Indian philosophical traditions of the Buddha's time so he did not teach them openly. Such *sang ngag*, or secret mantra teachings, are also described as hidden both because they are internally applied and because they are not widely taught even today. Why are they kept secret? It is not because they have faults, but rather because they are very powerful and beginning practitioners do not have the capability to benefit from these teachings immediately. If practitioners who do have the capabilities receive the detailed instructions from a qualified teacher and practice accordingly, they will have a special opportunity to swiftly realize their true nature.

The teachings on the channels, winds, and essences (or *tsa, lung, thigle*) are a vast system of knowledge, much of which is very intricate. What we present here is like a root text. It is simply the briefest outline of each practice.[50] In order to actually do these practices, a student will need to obtain extensive instruction from a qualified teacher. Such instructions are offered to a student who is found to be ready and given individually and in private.

What is required in order to be ready? We must first have established a firm foundation in basic shamatha (calm abiding) and bodhichitta practices, a good understanding of emptiness, and a basis in *Trekchö*.[51] Without these, the strong blissful sensations encountered in the secret practices may arouse extremely strong grasping and clinging which might become powerful obstacles. It would be harmful to our progress to cling even to a good meditation experience. However, with a strong basis we will be prepared to transform these experiences into realization.

The Practice of the Ultimate Meaning

The ultimate (or most secret) meaning is the meaning according to the view and practice of the Great Perfection, or Atiyoga, "the completion stage without concepts." At this level, we practice on the three vajra states of Tara: vajra body, vajra speech, and vajra mind.[52] What is meant by practicing on the three vajra states? When we meditate like this, all the forms we see, whether objects of the eye or eye consciousnesses, are seen as none other than the vajra form of Tara. All the elemental sounds that we hear are understood to be none other than the mantra, or the vajra sound, of Tara. All our thoughts, our mental formations, are recognized as none other than the supreme pervasive mind of Tara, the state of openness, spaciousness, and transparency. There is nothing else other than this!

These three vajra states are not only to be practiced during sitting periods but at any time, such as when we are walking outside in the yard, under the trees, or on the road. In practicing like this we come back to our original true nature. Cultivating this understanding, we sit, we walk, we wash dishes, or whatever activity is at hand. If we have that understanding now, that's great. If not, maybe trying it will bring a glimpse once in a while, like magic; that is known as understanding the nature of phenomena as magical display.

PART THREE

Detailed Commentary on
The Twenty-one Praises to Tara

Tara statue in the Gonpa at Padma Samye Ling

Introductory Homage to Tara

The Praises to the Twenty-one Taras begin with a special line of homage.

།ཨོཾ་རྗེ་བཙུན་མ་འཕགས་མ་སྒྲོལ་མ་ལ་ཕྱག་འཚལ་ལོ།

OM   JE TSÜN MA PHAG MA DRÖL MA LA CHAG TSHAL LO

OM   Homage to Noble Lady Tara.

In ancient times when the great masters translated a text from Sanskrit into Tibetan, they always put their own personal expression of homage and devotion at the beginning. Thus the words of this line are not part of the tantra itself. They were written by the original translator.

Next is an introductory verse, also not from the tantra.

།ཕྱག་འཚལ་ཏཱ་རེ་མྱུར་མ་དཔའ་མོ།

CHAG TSHAL TA RE NYUR MA PA MO

Homage to Tara, quick one, heroine.

།ཏུཏྟཱ་ར་ཡིས་འཇིགས་པ་སེལ་མ།

TU TA RA YI JIG PA SEL MA

With TUTTARA, you are the one who banishes all fear.

།ཏུ་རེས་དོན་ཀུན་སྦྱིན་པས་སྒྲོལ་མ།

TU RE DÖN KÜN JIN PE DRÖL MA
With TURE, the liberator who bestows all benefits.

།སུ་ཧཱའི་ཡི་གེས་མཆོད་ལ་འདུད་དོ།

SO HE YI GE CHÖ LA DÜ DO
With SOHA, I pay homage to you.

This preliminary verse serves to give a summary of the meaning of the ten-syllable mantra of Tara. In Tibet every school uses this preliminary verse and sometimes they chant it and sometimes not.

1. NOBLE LADY TARA NYURMA PAMO

Now we begin the actual tantra of Tara. The name of the first Tara, with all her Tibetan titles, is *Jetsün Drölma Nyurma Pamo*. In English her name means "liberator, swift one, heroine."

།ཕྱག་འཚལ་སྒྲོལ་མ་མྱུར་མ་དཔའ་མོ།

(1) CHAG TSHAL DRÖL MA NYUR MA PA MO
Homage, Tara, quick one,

།སྤྱན་ནི་སྐད་ཅིག་གློག་དང་འདྲ་མ།

CHEN NI KE CHIG LOG DANG DRA MA
Heroine whose eyes flash like lightning.

།འཇིག་རྟེན་གསུམ་མགོན་ཆུ་སྐྱེས་ཞལ་གྱི།

JIG TEN SUM GÖN CHU CHE ZHAL JI
Born from the opening corolla of the lotus face

།གེ་སར་བྱེ་བ་ལས་ནི་བྱུང་མ།

GE SAR JE WA LE NI JUNG MA
Of the lord of the triple world.

WORD MEANING

Jetsün in Tibetan is an honorific used for both men and women. Oftentimes for male buddhas it is translated as "Lord." For Tara, since she is female, we say "Lady." Jetsün [rje btsun] is composed of *Je* which means "supreme one, protector," and *tsün pa*, indicating a special or unique quality of body, speech, and mind. This word is applied in Tibetan to both male and female buddhas, for example Jetsün Jampal Dorje or Lord Manjushri; Jetsün Drölma or Lady Tara; and Jetsün Chenrezig or Lord Avalokiteshvara.

Drölma is translated as "liberator" or sometimes "savioress." What does "liberator" really mean here? By the activity of love and compassion, Tara is liberating all living beings from suffering, from fear, and from the miserable conditions of their samsaric existence, leading them to joy, peace, and the enlightened state. The Sanskrit Tara, the Tibetan Drölma, and the English "liberator" all share this meaning.

The third word, *Nyurma,* shows when Tara acts. Tara's compassionate activity is so quick, so swift! There is no delay, no sitting in the waiting room. I think she is quicker than 911!

The fourth name, *Pamo,* is the feminine form of the term for a hero, translated into English as "heroine." Pamo shows Tara's heroic courage and commitment to the liberation of all beings. She's not going to play at being heroic for a few days, then next month drop the project. She has a continuously heroic nature—never tired, never bored. Whatever difficulties arise, she continues working for all living beings. In summary, the name Drölma Nyurma Pamo, or Liberator, Quick One, Heroine, shows Tara's love, compassion, and power.

Even with these qualities, if wisdom were lacking she couldn't effectively liberate beings. Therefore, the second line of homage, "whose eyes flash like lightning," praises Tara's wisdom. We should not interpret "eyes" too literally. This is a metaphor for her third eye, which has the power of wisdom. Tara understands everything, in both external and internal realities, so she is able to truly help sentient beings swiftly and heroically.

The third and fourth lines, "Born from the opening corolla of the lotus face of the lord of the triple world," describe the source from which Tara emanated. One of the stories we mentioned before tells that Tara appeared in a tear from Avalokiteshvara's right eye as an expression of his supreme love and compassion. The term in the original Sanskrit was Lokeshvara, or Avalokiteshvara, who is Chenrezig in Tibetan. His title in Tibetan is *Jigten Sumgön,* which means "Lord of the Triple Worlds." What, then is the Lord of the Triple Worlds? None other than true love and compassion! In these last two lines, then, Buddha is praising Tara, saying in a way, "You emanated from love and compassion, you are working for sentient beings with love and compassion, and you yourself are the true embodiment of love and compassion, ability and wisdom. Mother Tara; I pay you homage."

GENERAL MEANING

The general meaning, an instruction on kye rim (or development stage) practice, tells us how we should visualize and meditate on Tara. We begin by visualizing Tara right in front of us. Once this visualization of Tara becomes stable, we may visualize her dissolving into ourselves so that we then become as Tara. Those are the two stages, or steps, of the visualization.

Now, let us go to specific details about the practice. As was discussed earlier, when we do the meditation of Tara or any other practice, our preliminary step should always be the same. It is to develop great bodhichitta by recalling the four immeasurables: boundless love, compassion, joy, and equanimity. This enlivens our loving and compassionate thoughts. We should also recultivate our joy and appreciation for our practice; it's not just an accident that we have this opportunity to be on our cushion and engage in this practice! It's truly a beautiful, special moment.

Next, chant the "Seven-Line Prayer" to Guru Padmasambhava three times and then the "Supplication to the Lineage Masters." This invocation is also a very beautiful praise to the Buddha. Remember that the practice of Tara comes from Buddha Shakyamuni; if Buddha

Shakyamuni had never appeared in this universe, we humans would never have experienced this form of teaching. Therefore, we give praise to the Buddha, the source of the teachings; to Guru Padmasambhava, who brought the teachings to Tibet; and to all the lineage masters that have shared and preserved them to this day. That is the motivation with which we chant the "Seven-Line Prayer."

Then we begin the actual visualization. In the first stage we should begin by seeing our surroundings and this entire universe as Lady Tara's pure land of Potala. It is marvelously beautiful; its beauty arises from the true nature of bodhichitta. Appreciate the beauty of this vision while visualizing the entire universe as Potala.

Now we begin to visualize a lotus seat and upon it a white moon disc, upon which Tara is seated in the royal ease posture.[53] Her face and body are red in color and her facial expression is semiwrathful. That means she is smiling, but fiercely, with her teeth showing. Her eyes are wide-open, round, and flashing a little bit like fire or lightning. Her right hand is in the supreme bestowing mudra. Her left hand is in the protection, or three jewels, mudra. With this mudra she holds the stalk or stem of a blue utpala (lotus flower), with the thumb and ring finger of her left hand toward her heart center. The open flower is at her left shoulder level.

Upon the pistil in the center of the open flower we should visualize a white conch shell,[54] which symbolizes the teaching of the Buddha. Imagine that Tara's conch shell is self-blowing or self-sounding. The self-sound of the conch is the sound of love, joy, and compassion; it is also a soothing, relaxing voice. The conch sounds words of welcome and consolation, words that give us hope, vision, and a clearer understanding into our troubles. By hearing the self-sound of the white conch, all our basic qualities of buddha-nature are aroused. We experience healing, which totally relaxes our anxieties and satisfies us. Be clear that the conch's sound, and the power and light of Tara's love and compassion, are not just for us practitioners but also extend to all living beings without any exception. Feel that every being is having a healing experience similar to ours. Continue in that meditation while reciting the ten-syllable mantra of Tara, OM TARE TUTTARE TURE SOHA, for as long as possible.

To conclude our visualization, Tara and her pure land are dissolved into the TAM syllable in her heart. The TAM syllable then dissolves into a very small dark red light. That red light finally dissolves into our heart center. Once in our heart center, Tara merges into our own true nature of being, or buddha-nature. We meditate in this state of natural awareness for as long as we are able.

To conclude this practice we dedicate the merit. For example, we can use *A Small Treasury of Prayers of Supplication and Dedication*,[55] which are all prayers written by the great masters. These are blessed words so we chant as many as we have time for. The dedication completes our practice of visualization, the general meaning. Apply these steps or stages, making the appropriate variations in the specific details of color, hand object, and so forth, to the practice of each of the twenty-one Taras.

HIDDEN MEANING

As discussed earlier, the hidden, or secret, meanings of these Praises to Tara contain symbolic or metaphoric instructions on the yogas of the physical body's channels, winds, and essences, or tsa, lung, and thigle. The yogic practices require extensive preparation and highly detailed instruction which do not fall within the scope of this commentary. What we will offer is just a brief summary, somewhat like a root text, for each practice.

The hidden meaning in this verse is based on three sets of three-fold realities. One triad is the relative body, speech, and mind. Another is the triad of the subtle or vajra body—its channels, winds, and essence elements. Furthermore, the subtle body has three main channels, the center, right, and left channels. The center channel is known in Tibetan as *tsa u ma* or in Sanskrit as *avadhuti*. In this context Tara's name Drölma Nyurma Pamo, or "Liberator, Quick One, Heroine," symbolizes the channels, winds, and essence elements of the body. The central channel is the Liberator, the winds are the

Quick Ones, and the essences are the Heroines.

The practitioner who has received instructions on the channels, winds, and essence elements will practice to move the winds and essences into the three channels and ultimately to establish all three—channels, winds, essences—within the center channel. At that moment he or she becomes like Avalokiteshvara or Tara with the "lotus face" of the totally awakened state.

By attaining this understanding of one's own physical body as the vajra body, one reveals the ultimate state of Tara, the swift and heroic liberator. And that is the totally awakened state, the state of absolute love, compassion, and wisdom. To that Tara we pay our inward or secret homage.

ULTIMATE MEANING

The center channel is also called by the Tibetan term Jigten Sumgön, or Lord of the Triple Worlds. At the ultimate level this Jigten Sumgön is none other than one's own true innate awareness, which in the Dzogchen teachings is called *rigpa*. Rigpa is the ultimate protector of all beings of the three universes.

After we receive instructions and undertake to practice in the Dzogchen way, we begin the process of uncovering our innate awareness, or rigpa. At the moment we realize this rigpa we spontaneously discover our liberated, quick, and heroic qualities. These three qualities are none other than the dharmakaya, sambhogakaya, and nirmanakaya states. In the Dzogchen teachings it is often said that the essential emptiness of the true nature is known as the dharmakaya, the clear light aspect of the true nature is known as the sambhogakaya, and the unceasing energy of the rigpa radiating to every direction is known as the nirmanakaya. These three kayas are the inherent qualities of rigpa, the state of true awareness, which is none other than Mother Tara's ultimate nature. And so we are paying homage to the ultimate Tara who goes beyond any mundane level of conceptions, who is self-inherent within us. We are paying homage to nonduality. That is the ultimate meaning of these four lines.

2. NOBLE LADY TARA
LOTER YANGCHENMA

The second emanation of Tara is named *Loter Yangchenma*. *Loter* means "knowledge-giver." The Tibetan term *Yangchenma* means "melodious, one who possesses melodies" or "source of melodies." So we might call her Drölma Loter Yangchenma: Melodious Liberator, Source of Wisdom. In Sanskrit she is called both Sarasvati and Vajrasarasvati. The Praise to Loter Yangchenma, or Vajrasarasvati, is:

།ཕྱག་འཚལ་སྟོན་ཀའི་ཟླ་བ་ཀུན་ཏུ།

(2) **CHAG TSHAL TÖN KE DA WA KÜN TU**
Homage, Mother whose face is filled

།གང་བ་བརྒྱ་ནི་བརྩེགས་པའི་ཞལ་མ།

GANG WA JA NI TSEG PE ZHAL MA
With the light of an array of a hundred full autumn moons,

།སྐར་མ་སྟོང་ཕྲག་ཚོགས་པ་རྣམས་ཀྱིས།

KAR MA TONG THRAG TSHOG PA NAM CHI
Shining with the brilliant open light

།རབ་ཏུ་ཕྱེ་བའི་འོད་རབ་འབར་མ།

RAB TU CHE WE Ö RAB BAR MA
Of the hosts of a thousand stars.

WORD MEANING

First, recall that the characteristics of liberty, swiftness, and hero-ism, as well as love and compassion, apply to every emanation of Tara. We want to remember to apply those to each of the Taras.

Buddha praised Vajrasarasvati as an embodiment of all that is beautiful. Anything we perceive that is beautiful, such as a beauti-ful work of art or a lovely melody, is a manifestation of the energy of Vajrasarasvati. To express this, Buddha praised Tara with the beauty of "an array of a hundred full autumn moons." Among all the moons of the year, the autumn moon is specially bright and clear in India and Tibet. In the dry, windy wintertime the moon is dulled by the "earth dust," and in the summer rainy season it is veiled by the "water dust," so at those times we rarely see its full brightness. But in autumn, when the sky is free from the two dusts, the moon is espe-cially beautiful. Thus the autumn moon is often used as the metaphor for white, rich, brilliant, and beautiful things. And here one moon is not enough; Buddha evokes the image of a hundred harvest moons. Here we should not fasten on a literal number, but imagine countless brilliant moons as an example of Vajrasarasvati's immeasurable knowledge. We might paraphrase Buddha's words in this Praise as follows: "Your beauty, splendor, and magnificence, Va-jrasarasvati, shimmer with the light of wisdom like the stars. Your wisdom shines in every direction as stars shine around the moon. To you, Sarasvati, I pay homage."

GENERAL MEANING

The general meaning teaches us to use the method of generating visualization. The power of Buddha's teaching is that it is not just an intellectual exercise, not just for studying and discussing and ana-lyzing details. It teaches specific practices and meditations skillfully designed to help us discover the true nature of ourselves and others.

There are various emanations of Vajrasarasvati in at least five dif-ferent colors. In this Praise, the color of Vajrasarasvati's body is white. Many ancient masters, such as Longchenpa[56] and Tsongkhapa,[57] wrote praises to her as the symbol of beauty, art, and music, using poetic images of autumn moons and shimmering stars. They also used the sacred Mount Kailash as a metaphor, comparing the holy mountain's beauty, splendor, and qualities with the glories of a vision of Vajrasarasvati in all her splendor.

Our practice should begin, as before, with the supplication to Guru Padmasambhava and the lineage masters, while we develop our precious motivation of bodhichitta, our joy and appreciation, and our feeling of closeness to the Buddha, Dharma, Sangha, and Tara. As we begin to visualize Vajrasarasvati, we see all our surroundings as her pure land, the Potala. In the middle of the Potala we should see a lotus and moon disc. Upon the moon disc sits Vajrasarasvati, with one head, two arms, and two legs. Her appearance is exactly the same as that of Green Tara, but she is a very rich white, symbolizing her activity of pacifying. She is as white as the light of a hundred thousand autumn moons together—so white! and shining beautifully. She displays the same mudras as described before and her left hand is holding a flower stalk with a blue utpala flower opening next to her ear. On the pistil of the utpala flower we visualize a ritual mirror, a melong,[58] in which all wisdom is completely reflected. There's nothing either in front of or behind Tara that's not reflected in her mirror. In the center of the mirror we should visualize the HRING syllable, white and radiating white light in every direction.

With that visualization we begin to recite the ten-syllable mantra of Tara continually. From her heart, and also from the HRING syllable in the center of the mirror, light emanates to the ten directions. The light dispels all ignorance, gathers all the knowledge and wisdom that can benefit sentient beings, and returns back to the mirror. Then again from the mirror, light and wisdom radiate, filling every part of our bodies. We are completely filled with wisdom, love, and compassion. We ourselves begin to glow bright as sunshine. We become beings of light. Visualizing in this way, full of joy and bodhichitta, reciting the mantra continually, is how to practice Vajrasarasvati, or Drölma Loter Yangchenma.

Reciting Tara's mantra develops in us four different forms of knowledge. In Tibetan, we call these *so so yang dag pa'i rigpa zhi.* In rough translation, *so so* means "individual," *yang dag pa'i* means "truly, perfectly," *rigpa* means "knowledge" or "wisdom,"[59] and *zhi* means "four." Thus, this phrase means "four individual truly perfect wisdoms." These are: *dön*, the knowledge that accurately understands the definitive meanings; *chö*, the knowledge that understands all phenomena, or dharmas; *nge pa'i tsig*, the knowledge or wisdom that understands language or words; and *pob pa*, the knowledge of ready speech that, by understanding the capacities of beings, empowers one to teach with courageous eloquence.

Let us go a little deeper into these four perfect wisdoms of speech. The first knowledge includes not only the speech of human beings, but also the languages of animals and birds and the sounds of air, fire, water, and earth. It includes every sound that our ears can hear. The phenomenal or dharma meaning refers to a correct understanding of the interrelationships or balance of all natural systems. The third knowledge goes deeper. With it we have an accurate knowledge of the meaning behind all of these sounds without misunderstanding or misinterpretation. This knowledge expands our wisdom so that we come to understand the literal sounds of rain and wind, meanings of all natural sounds, the cries of animals, and the words of all human languages. Lastly, with the knowledge of teaching we have a definitive compassionate understanding of every individual's capacities and abilities. We are now ready to share our four knowledges—what we've heard and what we've learned. We recite Tara's mantra with the aspiration to develop these four knowledges.

Finally, we dissolve our visualization of Tara into the natural state and meditate as long as possible. At the end we dedicate the merit of our practice for the benefit of all sentient beings.

HIDDEN MEANING

In the Vajrayana teachings on the vajra body, the essence of the white element[60] resides within the crown chakra. The secret meaning hidden within this Praise to Loter Yangchenma is the instruction on expansion and movement of the white element through the five chakras and all the channels of the vajra body. The second line, "With the light of an array of a hundred full autumn moons," indicates the crown chakra. The third and fourth lines, "Shining with the brilliant open light of the hosts of a thousand stars," refer to the practice of continually expanding, sparking, and radiating the vital white element throughout every part of the channels and nerve systems. One must retain all of this great blissfulness and vitality and not release any of it externally. One must continue applying, reshaping, and expanding it, until reaching the state of coemergent great bliss-emptiness, or enlightenment. These are the practices by which one inwardly understands the nature of Loter Yangchenma.

ULTIMATE MEANING

At the Dzogchen level, "With the light of an array of a hundred full autumn moons" describes rigpa, the innate awareness state. It illustrates rigpa's intrinsic brightness, clearness, and purity. From beginningless time until now, rigpa has never been obscured—it is innately shining and radiant. The ultimate state of Vajrasarasvati is brilliant, pure rigpa.

Once we realize rigpa, clear and brilliant as the beams of the autumn moon, then our brightness is not limited to just one nugget. We are totally pervaded with rigpa's glowing energy, symbolized by the thousands of shimmering stars. So the shimmering of the stars, at the ultimate level, is none other than the shimmering of love, compassion, wisdom, courage, and commitment radiating beneficial activities to all sentient beings. When we recognize our rigpa, we too achieve the state of Loter Yangchenma and become able to benefit every living being.

There have been many great masters who have discovered the ultimate state of rigpa. Many of them, especially in the Nyingma School, didn't necessarily go to college. They ignored the rules of academic systems. But by going beyond boundaries and limitations, they revealed the ultimate autumn moonlike rigpa state and their knowledge expanded like the innumerable shimmering stars. These great masters are our witnesses that this can happen.

One leading example is Jigme Lingpa. When we read his life story, we can see that he didn't really study anything very much. He studied a little bit of astrology and some basic grammar, and then he received a few lineage instructions on ritual ceremonies. That's about all the formal study that is documented in his life story. Instead, he devoted his effort to meditation and practice in caves. Three times he had visions of Longchenpa in the wisdom body. When he emerged from his cave, he'd gotten the Vajrayana equivalent of a B.A., M.A., and Ph.D. from Harvard University!

After receiving encouragement and instructions from the wisdom body of Longchenpa, Jigme Lingpa wrote a very famous book which deals with all nine yana teachings of Buddhist philosophy, all the way from basic Buddhism to Atiyoga. It's one of very few teachings of this type in Tibetan that is written from beginning to end as a poem.[61] All of the learned masters of Jigme Lingpa's day were attracted by this scholar who had composed such a beautiful work. When we read it, we too are moved by its beauty. His accomplishment was definitely a sign that he had discovered the ultimate Vajrasarasvati. When we ourselves discover this ultimate Vajrasarasvati, then our knowledge too expands beyond limits.

In summary, at the secret level Tara is none other than the vajra physical system of channels, winds, and essence elements. At the Dzogchen level she is none other than a display of one's own true nature of the mind. She is an innate, inherent quality, there to be revealed for the benefit of ourselves and all sentient beings.

3. NOBLE LADY TARA
SÖNAM TOBCHÉ

The third Tara is named *Tara Sönam Tobché*. *Sönam* means "merit." It's also often translated as "good fortune, prosperity" or even "luck." *Tob* is the Tibetan word which means "power, ability," and *ché* means "increasing." Roughly translated, "liberator, increasing the power of prosperity and ability of merit" is the word meaning of this Tara's name. Other very popular names for her are Vasudhari in Sanskrit and Norjünma in Tibetan. The effect of practicing on this Tara of prosperity is not just that we will acquire external or material wealth, but also that we will develop inner or spiritual wealth. By practicing on Tara Sönam Tobché, we can develop both forms of wealth. The verse of homage is as follows:

།ཕྱག་འཚལ་སེར་སྔོ་ཆུ་ནས་སྐྱེས་ཀྱིས།

(3) **CHAG TSHAL SER NGO CHU NE CHE CHI**
Homage, Mother, golden one,

།པདྨས་ཕྱག་ནི་རྣམ་པར་བརྒྱན་མ།

PE ME CHAG NI NAM PAR JEN MA
Her hand adorned with a blue lotus,

།སྦྱིན་པ་བརྩོན་འགྲུས་དཀའ་ཐུབ་ཞི་བ།

JIN PA TSÖN DRÜ KA THUB ZHI WA
Whose field of practice is generosity, effort,

།བཟོད་པ་བསམ་གཏན་སྤྱོད་ཡུལ་ཉིད་མ།

ZÖ PA SAM TEN CHÖ YÜL NYI MA
Austerity, calm, acceptance, and meditation.

WORD MEANING

Originally these Praises were written in Sanskrit. Because of the verse form and the word order, when the verse was translated into Tibetan there arose several possible interpretations of the first two lines and the syllables *ser ngo* (gold-blue). We teach that *ser*, or gold, is the color of Tara's body—a very special gold. Since she is the Tara of prosperity, gold is appropriate to her activity. Blue, or *ngo*, is the color of the lotus, her hand object.

The third and fourth lines explain what Tara Sönam Tobché really represents in terms of her achievements or realizations. What has Tara achieved? What is it that the Buddha is praising?

Tara has realized the six paramitas.[62] First, she has perfected the practice of *jin pa*, giving or transcendent generosity. Second, she has attained transcendent joyful effort, *tsön dru*. Third, she has attained *ka thub*, transcendent discipline and morality. Fourth, she has attained perfected calm, or *zhi wa* in Tibetan. Ego-clinging, duality, grasping, and all the emotions are completely purified. Therefore, the highest state of calm and peace is reached, the state of wisdom. Fifth, Tara has attained the highest state of *zöpa,* which is patience, acceptance, or tolerance. The sixth and last paramita is meditation or concentration, which is *samten* in Tibetan. Thus Buddha honors Tara as "You who have attained transcendent meditation."

One who has attained the six paramitas is known as a totally enlightened being. So, in brief, we can imagine we are hearing Buddha praising Tara Sönam Tobché as follows: "You, Tara, golden colored, and holding a blue lotus flower in your left hand, you who have accomplished all six paramitas, you who are a totally enlightened being, I offer praises to you!"

GENERAL MEANING

We begin the practice by developing love, compassion, joy, appreciation, and confidence. We offer devotion to all the lineage masters, buddhas, and bodhisattvas. Then we visualize the radiant pure land of Potala and a beautiful lotus and moon disc. Tara is sitting in a relaxing posture, with one head, two arms, and two legs. Her right hand is in the supreme giving mudra and her left hand is in the mudra called the protection, or three jewels, mudra, holding the blue lotus. She is very beautiful, embodying the love and compassion of all the buddhas and bodhisattvas of the three times. She is the rich gold color of Jambu River gold, *zambu chu ser*, gold melted and refined sixteen times. Her golden color symbolizes her activity of increasing. On the pistil in the center of the blue lotus we see a wish-fulfilling jewel, glowing and radiating all colors of light to us and all sentient beings. We continually recite the mantra of the ten syllables. With that, visualize the light from the jewel increasing merit and granting all wishes, particularly the bodhisattva vows of those who wish to benefit all living beings.

Then we dissolve everything into light into the TAM syllable, and then the TAM syllable dissolves into us. Now there is no separation between ourselves and Tara. In that state we meditate for as long as we have time. Afterward we dedicate the merit.

HIDDEN MEANING

The hidden meaning of this Praise contains instructions on increasing the inner heat, or *tummo*.[63] There are three important symbolic words in this Praise, the words lotus, gold, and blue. Tara's lotus, at the hidden level, symbolizes the secret chakra, and the secret chakra is the source of tummo and wisdom. Tara's hand, holding a lotus with the wish-fulfilling jewel, symbolizes skillful means.

Simply put, the inherent nature of one's inner heat is wisdom, and the visualization or method one uses to increase it is the skillful means. The secret chakra tummo wisdom, radiating heat or blissfulness, must join with the skillful means to increase its power. Practicing on the wisdom potential of the secret center, using skillful means, will bring increasing blissfulness, symbolized by the gold. If we combine skillful means and wisdom, then it is not possible that our progress to realization will slow down. This increasing blissfulness leads us to a complete understanding of emptiness, the un-changeable true nature symbolized by the color blue.

The six paramitas are our wealth. With increasing blissfulness one's wealth of the six paramitas can be increased. Increasing the great blissfulness energy, combined with wisdom, increases the en-ergy of generosity. There is also a great growth of joyful effort, with nothing that is selfish or personal in it. Don't misunderstand; this effort has nothing strained or forced about it. It's just joy, a moving force arising naturally. Maintaining the blissful state, totally relaxed but with discipline, increases the wealth of morality. Maintaining the mind totally steady and calm while in the blissful state increases the wealth of wisdom. Maintaining the totally tranquil state of shamatha increases the wealth of concentration or meditation. Fi-nally, continuing with strong qualities of commitment increases the wealth of patience. So, by these practices of the inner Tara Sönam Tobché, all six paramitas may be attained.

Remember that the Vajrayana path is based on the total union of wisdom and skillful means. If one follows it the right way, then en-lightenment will be found quite easily. Therefore, the Vajrayana teaching is always known as the swift path.

ULTIMATE MEANING

The word, general, and hidden meanings all involve mental focus on objects of the mind. With the ultimate meaning we go beyond mental objects, words, and concepts. In Vajrayana teaching, this is called completion stage practice without concepts because in prac-ticing this we complete every realization without missing anything. At this Dzogchen level, the lotus symbolizes rigpa. Although the lotus grows from mud, its blossom is never dirty or muddy, but always clean, fresh, and beautiful. Similarly rigpa is very clear, bright, and beauti-ful. Like the lotus, it is never obscured by any externals. Rigpa is de-scribed as *rangjung yeshe*, literally "self-born wisdom," a wisdom that just appears or arises. This wisdom is always fresh, and it is our own natural mind. Rigpa is the source of every external and internal prosperity and of the blessings of joy, peace, love, and compassion.

Rigpa is never separated from the energy of the six paramitas. In particular, the sixth paramita, the practice of transcendent wisdom, is really practicing to reveal the nature of rigpa. The six paramitas are all part of rigpa's display, so by revealing our rigpa, the inner natures of all six paramitas are then spontaneously revealed.

The nature of rigpa is sharing, giving, and generosity, and so that aspect is the paramita of generosity. Then, rigpa awareness maintained continuously is the paramita of discipline. And rigpa nature, unobscured and undefeated by any external circumstance, is the paramita of patience, or tolerance. Rigpa's ceaselessly arising, never-ending energy of love, compassion, and kindness is the paramita of joyful effort. Rigpa's inherently calm, peaceful state, undisturbed by emotions, is the paramita of concentration, or meditation. Rigpa's freedom from boundaries, limitations, habitual patterns, grasping, and clinging is the paramita of wisdom. Rigpa, then, is the ultimate, prosperity-increasing Tara, the Tara who grants all wealth.

4. NOBLE LADY TARA
TSUGTOR NAMGYALMA

The fourth Tara is known as *Tsugtor Namgyalma* in Tibetan, or sometimes *Tsugtor Nampar Gyalma*. In Sanskrit she is famous as Ushnishtavijaya. The term *tsugtor* in Tibetan or *ushnishta* in Sanskrit indicates the topknot upon the crown chakra of a buddha, which is one of the thirty-two major marks of a fully enlightened being. *Namgyal* or *vijaya* means "victorious one." Roughly translated, her names mean "victorious one of the top knot." The verse says:

ཕྱག་འཚལ་དེ་བཞིན་གཤེགས་པའི་གཙུག་ཏོར།

(4) CHAG TSHAL DE ZHIN SHEG PE TSUG TOR

Homage, Crown of Tathagata,

མཐའ་ཡས་རྣམ་པར་རྒྱལ་བ་སྤྱོད་མ།

THA YE NAM PAR JAL WA CHÖ MA

Her actions endlessly victorious,

མ་ལུས་ཕ་རོལ་ཕྱིན་པ་ཐོབ་པའི།

MA LÜ PHA RÖL CHIN PA THOB PE

Venerated by the sons of the conqueror

རྒྱལ་བའི་སྲས་ཀྱིས་ཤིན་ཏུ་བསྟེན་མ།

JAL WE SE CHI SHIN TU TEN MA

Who have attained every single perfection.

This particular Tara is renowned as the Tara of long life, with the ability to strengthen the life force, life energy, and vitality of all sentient beings. She is also renowned for protecting beings from *ngen dro*, that is, falling to take rebirth in unfavorable situations or lower realms. In the Nyingma School there are both Kama and Terma teachings on this Tara. There are also many in the other schools, Sakya, Kagyu, and Gelug. In the tradition of practice on Tsugtor Namgyalma, one prepares one thousand of each kind of offering, such as one thousand water bowls or lamps, for a large ceremony. Tara's mandala is placed in the center of the shrine room, displaying those thousands of different offerings around. All the monks and nuns gather for the practice and circumambulate with walking meditation, chanting Tara's long-life mantra. This may be performed twenty-four hours a day for many days, nonstop. It's a very powerful and blissful ritual.

Why is she called the Tara of the Top Knot, or Ushnishtavijaya? There is a legend that at one time, when Buddha Shakyamuni was teaching, Tara manifested right upon his crown chakra and spontaneously taught the Tara practice. Thus, she is named Ushnishta Tara.

Why is she famous for protecting against rebirth in the lower realms? There is a story about the experience of a mighty god named Tenpa residing in the Tushita heaven. Tushita heaven is one of the levels within the gods' realm. Even though the gods have all the luxuries, pleasures, and beautiful objects of enjoyment, the gods' realm is still within samsara, or cyclic existence. Gods can enjoy their delights only as long as their karmic life-force lasts. When their positive karma is used up, they will die and be forced to take rebirth in a lower realm, maybe even in a hell realm, wherever their karma impels them to be reborn.

The gods fully enjoy their luxurious lives from the time they are born until seven days before their deaths. There are always picnics and dancing and maybe daily trips to the beach, I think! Maybe it's like Hawaii! Lotuses and more lotuses, gardens and more gardens, parties and more parties—they enjoy their lives to the fullest until seven days before they pass. Then, in the last seven days they suddenly come to see that they are dying and they become aware, too late, that they are about to lose their opportunities of enjoyment. They begin to suffer, terribly, in a way they never suffered before. They foresee their future destinations. Their bodies rapidly undergo decay, and look old, and give off unpleasant smells. Suddenly their friends, the other gods and goddesses, reject them and won't come close. So the dying gods have a terrifying, lonely passage.

Now Tenpa was really distressed, because he had become aware, not only that he was dying, but that his next rebirth was going to be in the animal realm as a piglet. There seemed to be nothing he could do, so he went to Indra, and begged Indra, "Please, tell me some way out of this!" Indra said, "I can't do anything about it.[64] However, there is a fully enlightened being named the Buddha Shakyamuni, who is a friend of every being. Maybe he has the solution—you should go and ask him." So the dying god went to Buddha and asked him for help. Buddha instructed him to practice on Tara Ushnishtavijaya. He did her practice fervently for five days and was able to prevent his taking rebirth as a piglet in the animal realm. And, thus, this practice is for stopping lower births.

The famous Indian master Vasubandhu took Ushnishta as one of his main practices. He had vast numbers of students and followers who followed him everywhere to sit, meditate, study, and receive his teachings. If you have traveled in Nepal, you may have been to the famous stupa which marks the place where Vasubandhu passed into mahaparinirvana.[65] He traveled there for that purpose with thousands of his students. Just before he passed away, he chanted his Ushnishtavijaya practice many times. Then he announced, "Now is the time for my mahaparinirvana," so he chanted the practice backwards and entered mahaparinirvana.[66]

WORD MEANING

Because this Tara appeared in wisdom light on the Buddha's

crown chakra, she is named Ushnishta. "Her actions endlessly victorious" means she gives everyone protection from premature death and from the fear of taking rebirth in the lower realms, or undergoing adverse changes of our situation. She also gives protection from unvirtuous activities and disturbing emotions, so that is another reason why she is endlessly victorious.

The last line, "attained every single perfection," refers not only to the qualities of the sons of the conqueror, a phrase that means the bodhisattvas, but also to Tara and her realizations. So, as we saw with the previous Praise, Tara is truly a buddha because she has attained all the paramitas. Her realizations are also to be understood to refer to her perfection of the ten bhumis and five paths. "Venerated by the sons of the conqueror" tells us that all the buddhas, all the bodhisattvas, all the arhats, and all the practitioners venerate Tara as their Mother.

GENERAL MEANING

In the visualization practice, we start by developing our motivation as before and then visualize the lotus, moon disc, and Tara sitting there, with one face, two arms, and two legs. Tsugtor Namgyalma is a rich gold. Her gestures and ornamentation are the same as for every Tara. In this case, in the middle of the open lotus, which she is holding at the level of her shoulder, there is a vase of immortality, filled to overflowing with long-life nectar.[67] The nectar, or amrita, is the essence of all the pure elements and wisdoms. With this visualization, full of devotion and focused concentration, recite the ten-syllable mantra. While we recite, light and nectar overflow from the vase and pour into ourselves and all living beings. Tara's light and nectar revitalize our energy and life force and decrease the disorders of the elements and systems of our body, completely reestablishing perfect equanimity. Tara's blessing dispels the fear of losing our fortunate human birth and counteracts the causes of transference, or rebirth, in the lower realms.

HIDDEN MEANING

The hidden practice of Tsugtor Namgyalma concentrates on the channels, winds, and the white and the red essence elements,[68] or thigle, of our vajra body. The best accomplishing practice is to bring up all the essence elements to the crown chakra. That is, one puts the thigle first into the three main channels, then into the central channel, and then up into the crown chakra. This is the highest level of achievement of practicing on the elements.

There are two words with hidden meanings here, Ushnishta and Tathagata. Tathagata shows the starting point at the secret center, also known as the wisdom center or the true nature center. From there the thigle will be brought up all the way to the destination, the crown chakra (or ushnishta). Moving every essence element into the central channel, and then up to the crown chakra, will bring the state "endlessly victorious." This is victory over emotions and obstacles, a victory which brings samsara and nirvana into a nondual state. The ability to do this, not just for one minute but as a continual process, is the realization which "attains every single perfection" of the six paramitas, the ten wisdoms, and the ten wisdom winds.

ULTIMATE MEANING

The ultimate Dzogchen meaning goes beyond purpose and imagination to the expanse of self-arisen wisdom, rigpa. The Tathagata is none other than dharmadhatu, pure from the beginning (*ka dak*), unimpeded, and clear. Every beautiful thing is spontaneously inherent (*lhün drub*) within the unimpeded nature of *Tögal*[69] practice. "Attained every single perfection" means the ultimate experience or attainment of enlightened beings. This Ushnishta realization is the absolute union of Trekchö and Tögal. This is the highest practice, bringing ultimate realization of the true nature, pure from the beginning. The paths and bhumis are accomplished in one single stroke.

5. NOBLE LADY TARA
WANGDÜ RIGJÉ LHAMO

The fifth Tara is known as *Wangdü Rigjé Lhamo*. She is Kurukulle in Sanskrit and Rigjéma or Rigjé Lhamo in Tibetan. *Wangdü* means power of "gathering, summoning," or "magnetizing." We can think of it as attracting everything beneficial, to benefit all beings. *Rigjéma* means "she who precisely understands everything" and *Lhamo* is "divine lady." So she is known as the Tara who precisely understands the power of magnetizing.

Kurukulle's practice is very extensively taught throughout Tibetan Buddhism. She is often named the "Red Tara" because of her color. Her Praise is:

།ཕྱག་འཚལ་ཏུཏྟ་ར་ཧཱུྃ་ཡི་གེ།

(5) CHAG TSHAL TUT TA RA HUNG YI GE
Homage, Mother, filling all regions, sky, and the realm of desire

།འདོད་དང་ཕྱོགས་དང་ནམ་མཁའ་གང་མ།

DÖ DANG CHOG DANG NAM KHA GANG MA
With the sounds of TUTTARA and HUNG,

།འཇིག་རྟེན་བདུན་པོ་ཞབས་ཀྱིས་མནན་ཏེ།

JIG TEN DÜN PO ZHAB CHI NEN TE
Trampling the seven worlds with her feet,

།ལུས་པ་མེད་པར་འགུགས་པར་ནུས་མ།

LÜ PA ME PAR GUG PAR NÜ MA
Able to summon all before her.

WORD MEANING

The first line is Buddha's praise in terms of Tara's speech. HUNG[70] and TUTTARA are her magnetizing speech. At deeper levels her sound, her whole mantra, is so powerful and strong that it fills the entire universe. The phrase "trampling the seven worlds" shows this immense power and ability.

The entire universe of samsara may be said to be divided into three realms, which are the desire realm, the form realm, and the formless realm. You may also have heard the universe described in terms of the six realms: the three lower realms, human realm, demigod realm, and god realm. Here we encounter the classification "seven worlds," a less common way to explain the realms. The god realm is here divided into two parts, the form realm and the formless realm, altogether making seven. There is yet another way to explain the seven realms—gods' realm, nagas' realm, humans' realm, hungry ghosts' realm, asuras' realm, kinnaras' realm, and the spiritual world of the vidyadharas' realm. However, whichever system we use, Buddha emphasizes that all beings are in samsara— no matter who they are or where they are, it is all the same thing.

GENERAL MEANING

We develop our bodhichitta motivation, with joy and closeness. Then, with pure nonconceptual understanding of phenomena, we see Tara in the center of the lotus and moon disc. Rigjé Lhamo is a red color, symbolizing the activity of overpowering or magnetizing, and she holds a blue lotus flower. In the center of the lotus flower we should visualize a many-colored bow and arrow.[71] Reciting the ten-syllable mantra, we meditate that from Tara, as well as from her bow and arrow, red wisdom light is emanating to all directions. The light returns to us, drawing with it like a magnet every essence of wisdom and everything that can benefit beings, with love and compassion. With that thought, continually reciting the mantra, we practice on Rigjé Lhamo. Then we dissolve the visualization, meditate, and dedicate the merit the same as we always do.

HIDDEN MEANING

The hidden practice is the dissolving stage with focus. At this level TUTTARA means "passionate longing." In Tibetan this is *tummo.* What, again, is tummo? It is the vajra body's inner fire, so it is wrathful like the fire element. Tummo is powerful, tummo is longing, tummo is passionate. The syllable HUNG is the unchanging nature of great bliss. After receiving instructions, one practices with this passionate, wrathful inner energy, which has the indestructible nature of great bliss, expanding that energy throughout the body systems. In the vajra body, the seven worlds are the five chakras and the chakras of fire and wind. This practice continually expands the seven chakras and the spokes of the chakras. Eventually the expansion becomes an unchanging open state "that fills the sky," symbolizing that bliss pervades every aspect of the body. The entire universe is filled with great bliss and everything in all the realms transforms, attracted or magnetized into the wisdom of great bliss and emptiness.

ULTIMATE MEANING

According to Dzogchen, the mantra syllables HUNG and TUTTARA are teachings on the practices of Trekchö and Tögal. Through Trekchö and Tögal practices we liberate all longings and passions into rigpa, the innate self-awareness state. We can say that rigpa is TUTTARA and HUNG, or that TUTTARA and HUNG are rigpa. At the instant we recognize or understand rigpa, we see the three realms as the realms of body, speech, and mind, manifested as the three kaya states.

In this case the phrase "seven worlds" refers to the seven consciousness states,[72] which are transformed into wisdom states. All of our states of consciousness, perception, and conceptualization are transformed into wisdom energy. So we should view our seven consciousnesses not as obscurations, not as something to reject, but as the display of primordial wisdom which we have just rediscovered. The dharmadhatu, or great expanse, is filled with that wisdom display.

To meditate in that view is the ultimate practice on Wangdü Rigjé

Lhamo. The great masters say, "Once you understand the nature of mind and discover rigpa, then you have achieved the four buddha activities." This includes the magnetizing, overpowering activity. What have we overpowered? We have overpowered our own ego-clinging, our conceptions, and our emotions with the power of wisdom energy. There is no higher activity of attracting and overpowering than that; it is the ultimate accomplishment.

6. NOBLE LADY TARA
JIGJÉ CHENMO

The sixth Tara's name is *Jigjé Chenmo*. Now *Jigjé* means "fierce, frightening" and *Chenmo* means "great one," so this Tara is the great, fierce Tara. She is renowned for protecting against any negative force we feel is disturbing us, whether it is due to invisible beings and negativities or visible obstacles. Her Praise is:

།ཕྱག་འཚལ་བརྒྱ་བྱིན་མེ་ལྷ་ཚངས་པ།

(6) CHAG TSHAL JA JIN ME LHA TSHANG PA
Homage, Mother, worshipped by Indra, Agni, Brahma,

།རླུང་ལྷ་སྣ་ཚོགས་དབང་ཕྱུག་མཆོད་མ།

LUNG LHA NA TSHOG WANG CHUG CHÖ MA
By the Marut and different mighty ones.

།འབྱུང་པོ་རོ་ལངས་དྲི་ཟ་རྣམས་དང་།

JUNG PO RO LANG DRI ZA NAM DANG
Honored by the hosts of spirits, of yakshas,

།གནོད་སྦྱིན་ཚོགས་ཀྱིས་མདུན་ནས་བསྟོད་མ།

NÖ JIN TSHOG CHI DÜN NE TÖ MA
Of gandharvas and the walking dead.

WORD MEANING

The word meaning of this Praise is fairly straightforward. It tells us that Tara's abilities are so great that she can subdue all other mighty beings, whether they are worldly gods historically worshipped in India, such as Indra, or terrifying visible and invisible spirit beings such as the *rolangs*, or walking dead.[73] These "different mighty ones" are in reality none other than our own well-concealed internal obscurations and negativities, which take innumerable forms. Some of these we are able to see and some of them we don't know about at first.

GENERAL MEANING

With the supreme preparation and motivation, we should visualize Tara in the center of the lotus and moon disc, with one face, two arms, and two legs, in her usual posture. Her color is dark red, almost black, which symbolizes the activity of subjugating. On the pistil of the lotus she holds a black *phurba*, or dagger, which is sparking fire.[74] Her expression is semiwrathful. As we say the ten-syllable mantra, we should visualize flaming, sparking light radiating to all directions from her and from the phurba. When the light enters us, it removes all sorts of powerful obstacles and obscurations. Any mental negativity, especially delusion, insanity, and loss of memory, that bothers us is subjugated and removed. We think of that and recite the mantra, then we dissolve the visualization, merge the light to our heart center, and meditate on the true nature of great emptiness.

HIDDEN MEANING

This practice works with the vajra body's five elements and the winds of the five elements. The five elements are earth, water, fire, air, and sky or space. The winds of the elements are, therefore, the wind of earth, the wind of water, the wind of fire, the wind of air, and the wind of space. The winds of the elements are, then, the subtle essence energies of the elements. By practicing with these, we begin to understand the meaning of the five wisdom energies more clearly and strongly.

ULTIMATE MEANING

The ultimate meaning is based on understanding rigpa. When one recognizes rigpa, at that moment one has accomplished the male and female buddhas of the five Buddha families. They are all rigpa's display of the five wisdoms. So, once we discover rigpa and maintain that state, we are within the pure land of the five Dhyani Buddhas. By simply relaxing in rigpa, the mind's pure nature, we discover all the realizations of Tögal. Put another way, Tögal is none other than understanding everything within the display of the five wisdoms and the five Dhyani Buddhas. That is the ultimate meaning of this teaching.

7. NOBLE LADY TARA
ZHENGYI MITHUBMA

The seventh emanation of Tara is known as *Zhengyi Mithubma*. Her name means "unconquerable, cannot be defeated by others." Her Praise is:

།ཕྱག་འཚལ་ཏྲཊ་ཅེས་བྱ་དང་ཕཊ་ཀྱིས།

(7) CHAG TSHAL TRET CHE JA DANG PHET CHI
Homage, Mother, destroying the magical devices of outsiders

།ཕ་རོལ་འཕྲུལ་འཁོར་རབ་ཏུ་འཇོམས་མ།

PHA RÖL THRÜL KHOR RAB TU JOM MA
With the sounds of TRET and PHET,

།གཡས་བསྐུམ་གཡོན་བརྐྱང་ཞབས་ཀྱིས་མནན་ཏེ།

YE KUM YÖN JANG ZHAB CHI NEN TE
Trampling with her right leg bent and the left extended,

།མེ་འབར་འཁྲུག་པ་ཤིན་ཏུ་འབར་མ།

ME BAR THRUG PA SHIN TU BAR MA
Ablaze with a raging wildfire.

WORD MEANING

Here we are praising the power of Tara Zhengyi Mithubma's sound or speech of TRET and PHET,[75] with which she destroys all negativities. In Sanskrit the first syllable is TRATTA; in Tibetan we just say TRET, which means "completely flattened, smashed." PHET is also Sanskrit; it means to "split," or "totally cut through," stopping everything.

What is Zhengyi Mithubma smashing? What is she cutting? "Magical devices," sometimes translated as hex-wheels, are in Tibetan *thrül khor*. There are external thrül khor and internal thrül khor. *Thrül* as an adjective means "imitation" or, in a verb form, it means "trying to change something from its natural state." *Khor* means "wheel," which also suggests a continuous process; so *thrül khor* is a continuous, artificial activity. In Tibet, where there hasn't been much technology until recently, machinery in general is called *thrül khor* because it is not entirely natural.

Here the term refers to the internal thrül khor of our negativities and obstacles. Negativity—ignorance, anger, attachment, jealousy, doubt—is an artificial use of the mind and, unfortunately, for many beings it is continuous. The term *thrül khor* also includes overt external deeds by which we act out our negativities and attempt to deceive or take advantage of others. Furthermore, *thrül khor* also includes harmful internal ways of actualizing negativity by misuse of mantras, black magic, and spells. Such practices are aiming our spiritual powers totally in the wrong direction. All those types of action are indicated by *thrül khor*.

There are also two other ways to understand this term *thrül khor*. There are thrül khor of visible beings and thrül khor of invisible beings. We are quite familiar with the machines and devices of visible beings, such as human beings. However, there are also many sorts of invisible beings and they share many characteristics with us. For example, we believe that we humans "own" this world because we live here. But many invisible beings also have a similar attitude toward their territory and they think they "own" it. So there are many ownerships, not just one! If the invisible beings become uncomfortable and dissatisfied, they can make magical devices or obstacles, thrül khor, which reflect in external reality. We don't say that everything can be blamed on them, but sometimes they play a role in what we know as "accidents," as well as in natural disasters such as earthquakes, hurricanes, thunderstorms, and lightning. Whether it is a visible hex-wheel or an invisible thrül khor, whatever force is harming or disturbing beings, that is what this Tara stops or smashes.

The third line explains Tara's gestures and her attitude of splendor and majesty. "Trampling with her right leg bent and the left extended" describes her energetic but totally relaxed posture. She is both fierce and gracefully beautiful at the same time. The last line describes her majestic location within the raging wildfire, or wisdom fire. She is completely at ease and relaxed, yet actively trampling all the hard-to-tame negativities due to visible and invisible causes.

GENERAL MEANING

With bodhichitta and devotion, after saying the lineage prayers, we visualize Tara Zhengyi Mithubma on the lotus and moon disc with one face, two arms, and two legs. Her color is blue-black. She is described as being the color of heavy rain clouds or dense smoke. Her posture is the same as before, but she is sitting in flames of wisdom fire, surrounded with darkness. Her face has a frowning, wrathful expression. In the middle of the lotus flower which she holds in her left hand, there is a standing sword with a handle shaped like a vajra. Her sword flames and sparks fire.[76]

Despite her frightening appearance, Tara is still none other than true love, true compassion, and true wisdom, manifesting in a very powerful form. With that understanding, continually reciting the mantra, visualize wisdom lights and flame coming from her body and the sword. This blazing mass of wisdom energy removes all obscurations and smashes all thrül khor, both external and internal, due to visible and invisible beings. Think that all spells, curses, and delusions are completely cut through and stopped. At the end, we completely dissolve the visualization into light and into the TAM sylla-ble. We then dissolve the syllable into us and rest in the natural state of mind. Then we dedicate the merit for all beings.

HIDDEN MEANING

According to the hidden meaning of this teaching, both the right and left legs are relaxed. In saying "trampling with her right leg bent and the left extended," the two legs symbolize the two major side channels, right and left. The right leg bent means that the right channel is looking upward and the red element is ascending. The left leg extended means that the left channel is looking downward and the white element is descending. When a practitioner under-stands the secret method of controlling the upward and downward movements of the white and red elements, practice produces great inner heat, as explained here by "Ablaze with a raging wildfire." In the tantras it is said that this tummo fire comes from the short A syl-lable, the original, ultimate fire. By moving the two elements, the practitioner increases the intensity of this inner fire.

With this inner heat one can "destroy the magical devices of out-siders," which are the delusions of duality and conceptions. These will be completely smashed. Not only that, but by this secret inner heat practice one goes beyond the delusion of clinging to ordinary sensations. The mantra syllable TRET smashes ordinary sensations and the activity of clinging to them. One dissolves or goes beyond all attachments. The syllable PHET totally stops duality and cuts grasping motions. And that is the hidden meaning related to the vajra body.

ULTIMATE MEANING

According to the Dzogchen teaching, this blazing fire is primor-dial wisdom, or rigpa. "Trampling with her right leg bent and the left extended" symbolizes that hopes and fears are completely de-stroyed or transcended within the primordial wisdom state. When we hope, we are kind of looking forward into the future, thus her left leg is extended. When we fear, we are looking behind us, kind of tense or contracted, as shown by her right leg bent in. When we understand rigpa, we go beyond hope and fear. At that point there is no distinction between good and bad, gain and loss, samsara and nirvana. Every discursive notion collapses into the completely awakened state.

Just so, this TRET and PHET are used to stop hope and fear. Because the notions of samsara and nirvana merge in one single state, there is no more need for hope or fear. Using this metaphor, it says "destroying the magical devices of outsiders" to indicate our complete liberation of grasping and duality. The "hex-wheel" of doubt is destroyed. In fact, in the transformed view, our enemies become our great friends. The hex-wheels, or delusions, are now seen as a display of our inherent natural state so we don't have to be worried or concerned about them any more. They're recognized as perfect, "friendly" displays.

8. NOBLE LADY TARA
ZHENGYI MIGYALMA

Zhengyi Migyalma's name, roughly translated, means "invincible lady." You can't win against her. So, if you're a mara, or demon, better leave her alone! Or better yet, be nice to her. Her Praise is:

།ཕྱག་འཚལ་ཏུ་རེ་འཇིགས་པ་ཆེན་མོ།

(8) CHAG TSAL TU RE JIG PA CHEN MO
Homage, TURE, terrible lady,

།བདུད་ཀྱི་དཔའ་བོ་རྣམ་པར་འཇོམས་མ།

DÜ CHI PA WO NAM PAR JOM MA
Who annihilates the warriors of Mara,

།ཆུ་སྐྱེས་ཞལ་ནི་ཁྲོ་གཉེར་ལྡན་མཛད།

CHU CHE ZHAL NI THRO NYER DEN DZE
Slaying all enemies with a frown

།དགྲ་བོ་ཐམས་ཅད་མ་ལུས་གསོད་མ།

DRA WO THAM CHE MA LÜ SÖ MA
Of wrath on her lotus face.

WORD MEANING

The first line suggests her terrifying appearance. The second line, "annihilates the warriors of Mara," shows that Tara has the power and ability of a buddha. The mantra syllable TURE indicates that she is totally fearless in destroying the maras, or the fears. What are these fears? According to the Dzogchen view, all fears have to do with our mind. Every experience is the display of the mind and fears are no exception. Even though they are really nonexistent, we experience fears as nightmarishly real.

What can we say about these maras, these illusions? They are the monster creations of one's own imagination. These monsters are the illusory source of our fears. "Monsters" suggests what? Maybe something big, stubborn, and courageous, or maybe something very tiny but able to make big problems. So Tara Zhengyi Migyalma is not just destroying "marshmallow" demons; these are serious, solid demons. She's really a heroine.

Mara is a Sanskrit word which, roughly translated into English, means "demon" or "devil." Remember that as Buddha Shakyamuni sat under the bodhi tree, he was tempted by the maras, who tried unsuccessfully to prevent his attaining enlightenment. There are four principal demons, or maras: the Mara of Illusions, the Mara of Aggregates, the Mara of the Lord of Death, and the Mara of Distractions. This last one, the Mara of Distractions, is one of the worst maras, because it is quiet and sneaky. Buddha compared distractions to honey put on the sword, or an arrow of flowers, things that are seemingly attractive but actually have a disguised potential for great harm. Guru Rinpoche warned us that even good practitioners will often be challenged by this Mara of Distractions. Even if we have good realizations, we must be careful of the Distraction Mara. It could sneak up on us!

Zhengyi Migyalma's activity is to tame these four principal maras. "Frowning with wrath on her lotus face" shows her two aspects. While she is wrathfully subduing illusions, she wears a terrifying frown. But when she has finished destroying the maras, she is once again beautiful like a lotus, remaining strong and powerful. Thus, we can have confidence that although Tara is innately peaceful, loving, and kind, when necessary she will appear in this intensely powerful, fierce form to defeat all the forces that are hurting sentient beings.

At the mundane level, this Tara has special abilities to protect us against troublemakers, persons who criticize and harass others, and people who bring lawsuits.

GENERAL MEANING

After developing our motivation, we visualize Tara's color as a dark red. Her posture and gestures are the same as before. Here, in the center of the lotus, stands a flaming vajra.[77] While reciting the mantra continually, visualize that her body and the vajra on the lotus at her left shoulder are emanating a powerful blaze of wisdom light and flames, which burn up and destroy all obstacles and maras. Then, dissolving the visualization as before, meditate on the natural state and dedicate the merit.

HIDDEN MEANING

In this Praise, "Mara's warriors" symbolize the karmic winds. These karmic winds are very powerful. They distort our entire understanding and experience, leaving us with a deluded view of reality. With training on the tsa, lung, and thigle (channels, winds, and elements), the ultimate goal is to bring this karmic wind into the central channel, avadhuti. Then Mara's warriors will be totally destroyed. At that moment the great bliss-emptiness understanding will shine and grow. This is symbolized by Tara's lotus face frowning. It is the expanding great blissfulness energy obtained by practicing the tsa, lung, and thigle or by putting the impure karmic wind into the central channel. This attainment also releases all the knots of the channels. The knots are symbolically enemies, so by releasing them we "slay all enemies."

ULTIMATE MEANING

According to the Dzogchen meaning of this Praise, TURE, which means "swift" or "quick," refers to the fact that Dzogchen is the quickest path. When we are following the path of Dzogchen, meditating and practicing, the Dzogchen teaching is so powerful that it is "terrible" because it will transcend all the false hero maras. These are duality, conception, and emotions. There is no need for thoughts of rejection or acceptance because all impure thoughts become the display of the primordial wisdom and completely dissolve without a trace.

This is the spontaneously inherent awakening. There is no need to make any effort. Thus, the Dzogchen teaching is the practice that goes beyond effort and force. It will bring the ultimate understanding of rigpa, the true nature of the mind. That's the lotus face, grimacing with passion—totally awakened like the sun, free from all clouds and dust, beautifully shining in every direction.

9. Noble Lady Tara
Sengdeng Nagchi

Green Tara, who protects from all external fears, is named *Tara Sengdeng Nagchi* or sometimes *Sengdeng Nagchi Drölma*. The *sengdeng* is a very large tree, known as teak in English. Some trees are considered peaceful and others wrathful; sengdeng is known as a wrathful tree. In Tibet *damaru* and *chöd* drums are made from this strong, dense wood. So there are frequent references to sengdeng damaru. In Tibetan medicine the bark and resin are used to make a tea considered very beneficial for the blood. As *nag* means "forest," she is the Green Tara of the sengdeng forest. Her verse of homage is as follows:

།ཕྱག་འཚལ་དཀོན་མཆོག་གསུམ་མཚོན་ཕྱག་རྒྱའི།

(9) **CHAG TSHAL KÖN CHOG SUM TSHÖN CHAG JE**

Homage, Mother, her hand adorns her heart

།སོར་མོས་ཐུགས་ཀར་རྣམ་པར་བརྒྱན་མ།

SOR MÖ THUG KAR NAM PAR JEN MA

In a mudra that symbolizes the Three Jewels.

།མ་ལུས་ཕྱོགས་ཀྱི་འཁོར་ལོ་བརྒྱན་པའི།

MA LÜ CHOG CHI KHOR LO JEN PE

Adorned with the universal wheel,

།རང་གི་འོད་ཀྱི་ཚོགས་རྣམས་འཁྲུགས་མ།

RANG GI Ö CHI TSHOG NAM THRUG MA

She radiates turbulent light.

WORD MEANING

The first two lines call attention to Tara's gesture, or mudra. This "mudra that symbolizes the Three Jewels" is the mudra displayed not only by Sengdeng Nagchi Drölma but also by all the other Taras. It is also known as the protection mudra, so by praising this gesture of Tara's we are paying homage to her ability to protect from fears. How does she protect? With the "turbulent light" radiating from her palm which is marked with the universal wheel. Tara's love, compassion, and wisdom radiate and swirl unendingly, protecting every being in the ten directions from fear.

What are the eight great fears, according to Buddha's teaching? Because each fear has an outer, or physical, and an inner, or mental, manifestation, they are also referred to as the twofold eight fears. The first is described as the fear of elephants. Not only is a raging elephant physically very much to be feared, but the elephant also symbolizes the mental poison of ignorance. Thus we have a twofold fear—the external fear of elephants and the internal fear of ignorance. The second great fear is the fear of demonic forces, which in Tibet are called *shaza*, or cannibals. Demonic forces inwardly symbolize doubt. The third great fear is the fear of water and its associated inner fear, the ocean of desires. The fourth is the fear of fire, which at the inner level is the fear of anger. The fifth is the fear of robbers or bandits. That, at the inner level, is understood as the fear of wrong ideas and wrong beliefs. The sixth is the fear of poisonous snakes, which at the mental level is the fear of jealousy. The seventh is the fear of lions, the mental equivalent of which is the fear of pride or arrogance. And the eighth is the fear of chains, imprisonment, kings (or authority). These correspond to the inner imprisonment of attachments and greed. These, then, are the twofold eight great fears according to the Buddha. Tara the Heroine protects us from all of these fears and their causes. Briefly, then, Buddha is saying, "You, Sengdeng Nagchi Drölma, protect from all fears from the ten directions and the eight great fears. To you, great Mother, I pay homage."

GENERAL MEANING

First, we develop our motivation and say the introductory prayers. Then we visualize Sengdeng Nagchi Drölma as emerald green in color. In the center of the lotus in her hand, we should visualize the eight-spoked wheel of Dharma, radiating wisdom.[78] Reciting the ten-syllable mantra, continually visualize that from her body and the wheel radiate masses of turbulent beams of wisdom light to all beings. These beams protect us from adverse circumstances and eliminate all fears. We can also meditate that a vast number of dharma wheels emerge from her palm, one after another, and roll out in all directions to protect us and all other beings from every fear. Conclude by dissolving Tara into the seed syllable TAM, or into light, and then meditate in the pure nature state before dedicating the merit.

HIDDEN MEANING

According to the hidden meaning, this "mudra that symbolizes the Three Jewels" refers to the wind energy and the two subtle essences of the white element and the red element. These three components, according to the Vajrayana teachings, are the basis upon which we take rebirth and the basis of the lifespan. The consciousnesses are connected with the winds and the subtle essences of the white and the red elements. Because of the wind energy, consciousness moves continuously. The practice is to bring the wind and the two subtle essences together in order to actualize. "Her hand adorns her heart" symbolizes bringing those three components back to the heart center.

Now we're not going to be able to hold those three together at the heart center with duality! We need to bind them at the heart center in the nondual state and become "adorned" with wisdom and great blissfulness. Then wisdom, joy, and blissfulness "radiant with turbulent light" will spread in every direction throughout the chakra and channel system. Not only that—the entire universe will appear as the land of bliss. With that realization everything is transformed into the wisdom state. One is now able to protect every living being from difficulties, fears, and suffering, and to help other beings to progress on the path according to their capabilities, readiness, and needs.

ULTIMATE MEANING

According to the Dzogchen understanding, the mudra of the Three Jewels corresponds to the three vajra states: vajra body, vajra speech, and vajra mind. Once we discover our primordial wisdom and are able to effortlessly maintain that state, as it is, the three vajra states arise naturally. Nothing hides that reality from us.

What does "hand adorns her heart" mean here? It means that our realization will not come from outside. Realization is already within us, within our heart center. The primordial wisdom of the three vajra states is waiting to be discovered directly within our hearts. With the realization of the three vajra states, the eight great fears and the eight consciousnesses are transcended. Grasping is completely dissolved without any trace. In Dzogchen terms, that realization is known as *sa sum nam dröl*, "bringing the three worlds into the totally awakened state." In this way the three realms are liberated into their original natural state, as it is.

10. Noble Lady Tara
Jigten Sumlé Gyalma

The title *Jigten Sumlé Gyalma* means "Tara who gains victory over all the three worlds." Her special power is to protect us against distraction by worldly activities. Her verse of homage is:

༄༅།ཕྱག་འཚལ་རབ་ཏུ་དགའ་བ་བརྗིད་པའི།

(10) **CHAG TSHAL RAB TU GA WA JI PE**

Homage, Joyful Mother, whose brilliant diadem

།དབུ་རྒྱན་འོད་ཀྱི་ཕྲེང་བ་སྤེལ་མ།

UR JEN Ö CHI THRENG WA PEL MA

Spreads out garlands of light,

།བཞད་པ་རབ་བཞད་ཏུཊྚ་ར་ཡིས།

ZHE PA RAB ZHE TUT TA RA YI

Subjugating Mara and the world

།བདུད་དང་འཇིག་ཏེན་དབང་དུ་མཛད་མ།

DÜ DANG JIG TEN WANG DU DZE MA

With a mocking, laughing TUTTARA.

WORD MEANING

This Praise emphasizes Tara's inspiring mood. Not only is she joyous, but her joy and laughter bring others the same delight. The phrase "whose brilliant diadem spreads out garlands of light" means that whoever sees or has contact with her, or does her practice, will attain similar qualities.

In what way does her TUTTARA overpower the maras and other mighty ones? Her action of joyful laughter overpowers the mighty ones "of the world," which means she specifically protects us from those worldly things and activities which might prevent us from staying on the path of practice.

GENERAL MEANING

Start as always by developing the supreme attitude of devotion, appreciation, and bodhichitta. In the visualization, Tara's body is a rich, red color. In the middle of the blue lotus flower in her left hand there stands a victory banner.[79] When we achieve realization, we have won the great victory over our delusions. Reciting the ten-syllable mantra, see that from Tara's body and from the victory banner red wisdom lights emanate to the ten directions. By the power of her laughter, visualize that all the external mighty and arrogant ones are completely subdued. Our own internal "mighty one," our powerful arrogance or ego-clinging, is also subjugated into a gentle and peaceful state. Afterwards, dissolve the visualization, meditate in the natural state, and dedicate the merit for the benefit of all sentient beings.

HIDDEN MEANING

According to the hidden meaning, Tara's joyous delight symbolizes self-inherent blissfulness. Her garlands of light symbolize the white element, which is residing on the crown chakra, shimmering and emitting light in all directions. TUTTARA means powerful, passionate longing.

It is mentioned that there are eight different moods when Tara laughs. The method of this practice works with eight movements of the essences, related to Tara's eight ways of laughing, to increase bliss. This blissfulness is known as self-born bliss. It spreads in many radiant forms throughout the channel and chakra systems, waking everything up in great joy and, as it says here, bellowing laughter. The arising of the self-born bliss transforms all regular mundane pleasurable sensations which, under ordinary circumstances, give rise to attachment or clinging. These habits of attachment are the maras that are being overpowered in this case. These maras, or regular clinging sensations, arise based on the perceptions of ordinary body, speech, and mind. Therefore, the "three worlds" symbolize here the ordinary, obscuring view of body, speech, and mind, which are the obstacles that these practices destroy. They are replaced with the realization of vajra body, speech, and mind.

ULTIMATE MEANING

In the Dzogchen understanding, Tara's magnificent, joyous delight is the self-born awareness, or *rang jung yeshe*. First we recognize or are introduced to this self-born awareness. Then we apply the teachings and practice, and three different attainments come, one after the other. The first is a solid intellectual understanding of the self-born awareness. The second is a deepening experience of this rigpa, the self-born awareness. The third is complete realization of the self-born awareness. At this point we transmute and liberate all conceptions into the enlightened state, called here "subjugating Mara and the world." This realization is the true face of Mother Tara, or the true nature of the wisdom dakini, which liberates all phenomena into wisdom energy. Our old habits of grasping and ego-clinging are completely overpowered. Once we are freed from these obstructive habits, we can truly help other beings to subjugate their own obstacles. Then we too are in the state of Mother Jigten Sumlé Gyalma, who overpowers Mara and the world.

11. NOBLE LADY TARA
PHAGMA NORTER DRÖLMA

This eleventh Tara is named *Phagma Norter Drölma*. *Phagma* means "noble one" or "supreme one." Roughly translated, *Norter* means "bestowing riches," so Phagma Norter Drölma is the Noble Tara who bestows wealth. Her Praise says:

།ཕྱག་འཚལ་ས་གཞི་སྐྱོང་བའི་ཚོགས་རྣམས།

(11) CHAG TSHAL SA ZHI CHONG WE TSHOG NAM

Homage, Mother, able to summon before her

ཐམས་ཅད་འགུགས་པར་ནུས་མ་ཉིད་མ།

THAM CHE GUG PAR NÜ MA NYI MA

All the host of protectors of the earth.

།ཁྲོ་གཉེར་གཡོ་བའི་ཡི་གེ་ཧཱུྃ་གིས།

THRO NYER YO WE YI GE HUNG GI

Moving her frowning brows, she saves

།ཕོངས་པ་ཐམས་ཅད་རྣམ་པར་སྒྲོལ་མ།

PHONG PA THAM CHE NAM PAR DRÖL MA

From all poverty by the sound of HUNG.

WORD MEANING

The first two lines show Tara's summoning power, which is based upon her power of love, compassion, and wisdom. In her sovereignty she controls the host of protector deities called earth protectors. *Bhumipala* is the Sanskrit word for them; *bhumi* means "earth," and *pala* means "protector."

Who or what is summoned? The Goddess of Earth is the primary bhumipala who maintains the earth elements. In Tibetan, her name is *Sayi Lhamo Tenma Chenmo*. *Tenma* means "stable" and "firm," so her name means "great firm earth goddess." Additionally, there are ten bhumipalas related to the ten directions, each of which has a retinue.[80] Along with these bhumipalas and their retinues, Tara summons other gods renowned in ancient times, such as Indra, Brahma, and Vishnu. Through Tara's love, compassion, and wisdom, all the protectors of the ten directions, the goddess of earth, the ancient gods, and their followers become part of her retinue, under her control.

The next lines show another of Tara's wrathful appearances. As we have seen, sometimes Tara is very gentle and lovely and sometimes she can be very powerful and wrathful. Here she has a wrathful face, *thro nyer* in Tibetan. Now *thro* is "wrathful," and *nyer* means she has lines on her face—she's frowning. Her frowning brows, the sign of her wrathful energy, are moving while the powerful mantra syllable HUNG is sounding.

Tara Norter Drölma is renowned as Tara the wealth-giver, who removes the sufferings of poverty. With her intense wrathful energy, emanating the syllable HUNG in all directions, she showers down wealth, joy, and satisfaction to every single sentient being. This is not only physical wealth, such as plenty to eat and nice clothes and money. It is also the wealth of capabilities and understanding, which liberates beings from the poverty of ignorance. So her name is more fully understood as "Lady who liberates from every sort of poverty."

There is a beautiful story told about Tara and the great Indian master Chandragomin, who taught at Nalanda Monastery in the ancient times. He was a famous scholar, but very humble and poor, owning only his robes, bowl, and the text of the *Prajnaparamita*. One day a poor beggar woman came to him in tears, begging for a few alms so she could provide a dowry for her daughter. Having nothing of value to give her, Chandragomin began to cry. He prayed to a picture of Tara painted on the wall of his room. The image quickly came to life, took off her (now quite real) silken clothes and ornaments of gold and jewels, and gave them to him for the beggar woman's daughter. The painting then returned to his wall and was ever after known as the Naked Tara.

GENERAL MEANING

Let's pause to remind ourselves that the supreme bodhichitta intention is always necessary. We need joy and appreciation, devotion to Mother Tara, all the buddhas and bodhisattvas, lineage masters, and the teaching, plus respect for ourselves and our great potential. In these times we are all dealing with pressing and powerful worldly influences. Every one of us is intensely busy with all sorts of different activities. We often don't have enough time to do all the practice that we might wish. We might notice that our good habits are slipping away and we may get discouraged. Nevertheless, we must just come back and sit with good thoughts, restrengthening our beautiful motivations. Joyful effort, courage, and commitment will help us reevaluate the situation and bring ourselves back to the goal.

Starting our practice with the "Seven-Line Prayer," lineage prayers, and the motivation of bodhichitta and joy, again we visualize the lotus and moon disc. Upon it is Tara, who is orange or golden-red in color. She has one face, two arms, two legs, and her expression is a little semiwrathful. In the center of the lotus she holds a treasure vase filled with jewels,[81] which will grant all wishes. While reciting the ten-syllable mantra, visualize that from the vase, Tara's body, and her three places (head, throat, and heart chakras) radiate wisdom lights. These light rays have the activity of granting all wishes. As the light radiates out to us and all others and returns back, visualize that all the good things we wish for come to us. All of us are given a vast treasure of healthful, fortunate, and luxurious things. Tara also gives us the gifts of joy, peace, love, compassion, and enlightenment. Meditate on this, then dissolve the visualization, meditate in the pure nature state, and finally dedicate the merit.

HIDDEN MEANING

In the first line, in referring to the bhumipalas, or earth-protectors, the hidden meaning of "earth" refers to the lower, or secret, chakra. The lower chakra contains the essence, or thigle, we call the red element; it also can be thought of as a red molecule, or very subtle atom. The white element, or white molecule, is residing at the crown chakra. "Mother able to summon" means that the energy of the lower red element begins to bring down the upper white element. The white element is in a continual state of movement, expanding upward and downward. This practice of moving and expanding is protecting, or "pala." This means that by expanding the essences in their path and passages one is actually taking good care of them. The line about "frowning brows and the sound of HUNG" also symbolizes the movement of the white thigle up and down.

This practice mainly focuses on the location of what is called the "third eye." Images of the buddhas always show the third eye as a sort of small dot on the forehead above and between the regular two eyes. In this practice, all the essence elements are brought to that spot, where they begin to reveal their energy. "Frowning brows" means that the wrathful energy mainly appears in a visible way on the face. From this spot it begins to radiate, removing the poverty which is due to our lacking the knowledge of blissfulness and emptiness. We develop the subtle, unchanging "wealth" state of bliss-emptiness, completely removing this poverty. When this third eye spot is actualized, at that moment the sky-treasure samadhi, or space-treasure samadhi, is reached. Then every realization is achieved—there is nothing missing. This is the highest state of wealth. We can become a billionaire, or trillionaire, without worrying about any other applications!

ULTIMATE MEANING

In the Dzogchen teaching, "earth" or "bhumi" symbolizes the Ground, or Base. What is the ground of both samsara and nirvana? It is primordial wisdom or, in Dzogchen terms, rigpa. So rigpa is the ground from which everything emanates. Samsara and nirvana (the enlightened state) are not really distinct from each other. When we realize the rigpa nature, we are enlightened beings. When we don't realize this nature, we are in samsara. For that reason the "Prayer of Kuntuzangpo," from the *Unimpeded Realization Dzogchen Tantra*[82] by Padmasambhava, says, "If you recognize rigpa, you are enlightened beings. If you don't recognize it, you are deluded beings." So knowing and not knowing rigpa is really the borderline between enlightenment and delusion and between buddhas and sentient beings. Knowing rigpa, we reach enlightenment; not knowing rigpa, we stay deluded. So the "earth," or Ground in Dzogchen, is this innate awareness, rigpa.

It is also said that when we know this rigpa, then all its displays are understood. When we maintain our minds in the wisdom state, we are protecting the rigpa or "taking care of it." When we don't recognize that rigpa, our minds continue in the deluded state. In a way it might be said that we're maintaining and protecting. Unfortunately, this time it's the deluded state we're staying with. In either case we should be aware that we're maintaining something. But, knowing the essence of wisdom, we should always choose to try to maintain our awareness in the rigpa state. Once we understand rigpa, everything is in our hands. Nothing is beyond us. We become sovereigns of both samsara and nirvana, which are in one single state without any division.

12. Noble Lady Tara
Tashi Dönjé

Tara *Tashi Dönjé* means "Tara who actualizes auspiciousness." *Tashi* is the Tibetan word that means "auspicious circumstances," and *Dönjé* means "fulfilling" or "actualizing." In particular, this Tara is renowned for bringing harmony and balance. Internally she brings health and physical balance and externally she brings timely seasons, good harvests, healthy children, and prosperity. With her help all becomes as it should be. The verse of homage is:

།ཕྱག་འཚལ་ཟླ་བའི་དུམ་བུས་དབུ་རྒྱན།

(12) CHAG TSHAL DA WE DUM BÜ UR JEN
Homage, Mother, whose diadem

།བརྒྱན་པ་ཐམས་ཅད་ཤིན་ཏུ་འབར་མ།

JEN PA THAM CHE SHIN TU BAR MA
Is a crescent moon, blazing with all her ornaments,

རལ་པའི་ཁྲོད་ན་འོད་དཔག་མེད་ལས།

RAL PE TRÖ NA Ö PAG ME LE
Ever shining with the brilliant light

།རྟག་པར་ཤིན་ཏུ་འོད་རབ་མཛད་མ།

TAG PAR SHIN TU Ö RAB DZE MA
Of Amitabha in her piled hair.

WORD MEANING

The crescent moon in Tara's diadem (*dum bu* in Tibetan) is derived from a Sanskrit term which means "a piece of the moon." This corresponds to the seventh- or eighth-day moon in the lunar calendar. The light of that phase of the moon is said to have cooling energy. The Buddha taught that the dum bu showers a nectar of cooling and balancing energy in every direction, bringing perfect balance and auspiciousness. Disease, famine, and wars cease. The natural world becomes harmonious and enjoys the time known as a Golden Age.

The third and fourth lines tell us that Tara is none other than an emanation of the Buddha Amitabha, who appears seated in the hair piled or bound on her head, where he radiates beams of brilliant light. What is Amitabha's brilliant light? It's the inconceivable, powerful light of love, compassion, and wisdom, which brings auspicious circumstances of perfect joy, happiness, peace, and prosperity. Amitabha is a Sanskrit name translated into Tibetan as Ö pa me. "A" in Sanskrit is a negation and "mitabha" is light; all together the name means "immeasurable light." This light has the ability to remove the sufferings of beings and lead them to enlightenment. Here Amitabha, whose color is red as a ruby, is visualized particularly with Tara Tashi Dönjé. Generally, in Tara practices Amitabha is visualized in each of the Taras' hair or on their crown chakras. So it is correct to include him in every visualization of Tara if we wish.

GENERAL MEANING

First, we prepare ourselves by developing our motivation. In our visualization, Tara's color is golden yellow. In the center of the lotus is another of the eight auspicious symbols, the infinite knot or eternal knot standing upright[83]. It is in the form of light, as are all the objects on the lotuses in each of the visualizations of Tara. While reciting the mantra, visualize that from the eternal knot, Tara's body, the crescent moon, and the small ruby-red figure of Amitabha in Tara's hair, love, compassion, and wisdom radiate as blessing, cooling energy. This cooling energy removes all inauspicious circumstances, anger, and jealous attitudes. It rebalances all the elements of our earth. Whatever was unbalanced or reversed is reestablished so it can function as it should. External and internal forces, including mental patterns, become stabilized in an auspicious state of harmony and prosperity that fulfills every wish. Visualizing and meditating on that is the practice of Tara Tashi Dönjé.

HIDDEN MEANING

The crescent moon indicates the lunar or white element in the crown chakra, or the "white molecule." We should visualize it shaped as an inverted Tibetan syllable HANG.[84] Amitabha indicates the red element residing in the midst of her hair or her crown chakra. Normally, of course, the white element resides on the crown chakra and the red element is in the secret chakra. But, in this aspect of the secret practice, these two are brought together up through the central channel to the crown chakra. So when these two are bound together in union, without spoiling, decreasing, or misusing, then one understands the emptiness body of great bliss of Mahamudra.

ULTIMATE MEANING

Within the Dzogchen teachings, there are two main practices, Trekchö and Tögal. In the Tögal practices, different experiences or lights arise connected with our realizations. The first stage is "understanding clearly in direct perception reality as it is." The dum bu, or crescent moon, symbolizes this first stage of Tögal practice, *chö nyi ngön sum*. Then "blazing with all her ornaments" is the second stage of Tögal practice, known as *nyam nang gong phel*, or "expanding or developing the experience and realizations." The figure of Buddha Amitabha residing in the midst of Tara's hair symbolizes the third stage of realization, known as "reaching the peak of awareness," or *rigpa tse pheb*. Then the words "ever shining with the brilliant light" refer to the fourth, or ultimate, stage. It is called "concluding every conception into the true nature state," or *chö nyid ze sar*. This means everything is completely exhausted or liberated within the true nature state. The true nature state is beyond time; it always shines and radiates, as symbolized by these words, "ever shining with the brilliant light."

Ultimately one attains the transcendental wisdom rainbow body. These two stages, exhausting every phenomenal conception into the true nature state and attaining the transcendental wisdom rainbow body, come simultaneously. They are not separate, but are just different aspects of the realization. The transcendental wisdom rainbow body state is the result of exhausting every phenomenal conception into chö nyid, the true nature state.

13. NOBLE LADY TARA
YÜLLÉ GYALMA

This Tara's name in Tibetan, *Tara Yüllé Gyalma*, means "Tara who gains victory over war." She is renowned for protecting against all the obstacles related with wars. She can reverse the march of armies or stop the war completely. Her protection also applies inwardly, too, as she stops hostile emotions born of conceptual thinking that disturb our awareness and wisdom and might lead us to warlike actions. Her Praise is:

།ཕྱག་འཚལ་བསྐལ་པ་ཐ་མའི་མེ་ལྟར།

(13) CHAG TSHAL KAL PA THA ME ME TAR

Homage, Mother, residing amidst the garland that blazes

།འབར་བའི་ཕྲེང་བའི་དབུས་ན་གནས་མ།

BAR WE THRENG WE Ü NA NE MA

Like the fire at the end of the world era,

།གཡས་བརྐྱང་གཡོན་བསྐུམ་ཀུན་ནས་བསྐོར་དགའི།

YE CHANG YÖN KUM KÜN NE KOR GE

Right leg extended, left bent, encompassed by joy,

།དགྲ་ཡི་དཔུང་ནི་རྣམ་པར་འཇོམས་མ།

DRA YI PUNG NI NAM PAR JOM MA

Annihilating hosts of enemies.

Word Meaning

This Tara is praised as extremely wrathful. The first two lines locate her amidst a garland of wisdom fire "like the fire at the end of the world era." The Abhidharma describes the seven stages of destruction of the universe, by fire, water, and wind, after which this world will totally disappear. The first step of this destruction to come will be the biggest fire we can possibly imagine. These flames, powerful enough to destroy a universe, are a reflection of the great energy Tara can apply to her enlightened activities.

The third and fourth lines describe Tara's dancing movements. She's not just sitting within the wisdom flames, but she is dancing while she performs her beneficial activities to stop warfare. She's not acting out of sadness or suffering, but she's filled with joy and pleasure, dancing with her love and compassion for all. That is how she destroys the hordes of enemies and heals the destruction caused by anger, enemies, and war.

General Meaning

Start as always by developing the supreme motivation and chanting the "Seven Line Prayer." Visualize Tara sitting on the lotus and moon disc, this time in the midst of the blazing fire of the end of eons. Her color is dark red and her expression is wrathful. In the middle of the flower in her left hand there stands an open-pointed vajra.[85] Each point is flaming and sparking. With this visualization, reciting the ten-syllable mantra, meditate that from her body and from the vajra emanate flames and wisdom light. Tara's vajra emanates countless small vajras, each of which sparks and multiplies even more vajras in all directions. All the wars and destruction that harm sentient beings come to a stop. At that very moment everyone becomes joyous, peaceful, and relaxed. Then, all the vajras, having performed these wonders, return back and make a shield of protection for us, called a vajra tent. It gives us indestructible protection from negativities, obstacles, and disturbances. With these thoughts, recite the mantra, then dissolve, meditate, and dedicate the merit.

Hidden Meaning

This "Mother residing amidst the garland that blazes" symbolizes what in Sanskrit is known as a *chandali*. As we said before, in the Vajrayana teaching it is always necessary to know if a word is intended to be taken literally or whether it has hidden meaning. In this case if we translate this "blazing garland" literally as the Sanskrit word *chandali*, it comes out "cruel woman." But the real meaning isn't at all like that. It's a double meaning, a little pun. This cruel woman is a metaphor for the original fire, or tummo. She's so "cruel" because she destroys duality and disturbance. This chandali energy, or tummo, is the inner original wisdom fire based on total emptiness that resides within our vajra body.

The postures of Tara's right and left legs symbolize the upper subtle wind and the lower subtle wind. The secret practice on the subtle winds is used to release knots of the channels. At the moment of release one will be "encompassed by joy." When that status is achieved, the "hosts of enemies," the karmic winds of duality and conceptual thoughts, are defeated. These karmic wind energies are very strong; they control our vision, our attitude, and all our moods; they are unstable and shift quickly. Additionally, they influence our blood and all our other body systems. So when the capability to work with the wind systems has been developed, one destroys the karmic winds or duality winds by bringing them into the central channel.

Ultimate Meaning

In Tögal teaching, "blazing like the fire at the end of the world era" symbolizes original, unborn, and undying wisdom, which radiates all the time. This is the most powerful light. At this moment the undying flame of wisdom is hidden behind or within our phenomenal conceptions. This inner light resides within us, never dimming, never losing its qualities, never dying out. Whatever brightness, clarity, analytic energy, or understanding we have actually arise from that original, unborn wisdom. All are none other than the innate nature of our own mind. This wisdom nature of the mind is the ultimate fire that consumes all deluded perceptions. It is symbolized here by the fire at the end of the eons which burns up universes.

The right and left legs refer to two aspects of the radiating energy of our inner wisdom fire. The energy of true loving-kindness and compassion is united with the energy of wisdom. Together these energies guide and benefit all beings. If we develop understanding of our inner wisdom, we will totally transform all our neurotic and dualistic mental states.

14. NOBLE LADY TARA
THRONYER CHEN

This Tara is known as *Thronyer Chen*. *Thronyer* is "frowning, wrathful," so she is the very wrathful, frowning one. She is a special emanation of Tara whose activity is removing subtle obstacles due to misleading influences, which are usually our most stubborn obstacles. She deals with our last "wrinkles" or, we might say, the last two percent of our delusions, deep within the elemental nature of human beings. The verse says:

༁ྃ་ཕྱག་འཚལ་ས་གཞིའི་ངོས་ལ་ཕྱག་གི །

(14) CHAG TSHAL SA ZHI NGÖ LA CHAG GI

Homage, Mother who hits the earth with the palm of her hand,

༁ྃ་མཐིལ་གྱིས་བསྣུན་ཅིང་ཞབས་ཀྱིས་བརྡུང་མ། །

THIL JI NÜN CHING ZHAB CHI DUNG MA

Who pounds on it with her feet,

༁ྃ་ཁྲོ་གཉེར་ཅན་མཛད་ཡི་གེ་ཧཱུྃ་གིས། །

THRO NYER CHEN DZE YI GE HUNG GI

Frowning wrathfully, she shatters

༁ྃ་རིམ་པ་བདུན་པོ་རྣམས་ནི་འགེམས་མ། །

RIM PA DÜN PO NAM NI GEM MA

The seven underworlds by the sound of HUNG.

WORD MEANING

This verse shows that Tara does big things in simple, direct ways. The first two lines describe the power of her body. By slapping her hand on the ground and stamping her feet on the earth, she is able to shake the whole universe. The next two lines show the power of her speech. With the wrathful energy of the syllable HUNG she shakes all seven levels of the universe. She roots out and destroys all the subtle negativities caused by misleading, invisible influences.

GENERAL MEANING

In the visualization Tara's color is a dark, blackish, rain-cloud color; she is sitting on a lotus and moon, holding a blue lotus. On the flower is a *tung shing,* which is a grinding stick or pestle.[86] It's big, heavy, and made out of wood. You'll still see this in use in India, often with two men working together to grind nuts and seeds. It is also used for pounding mustard or sesame seeds to extract the oil. Remember the great master Tilopa, founder of the Kagyu lineage? *Til* is the word that means mustard seed or sesame seed in both Sanskrit and Tibetan. In Tilopa's life story we learn that he worked in a til factory, making sesame oil for the rich people. People named him Tilopa, the one who crushed the til. He was a great yogi and highly realized being, so while he was doing this humble work he was also meditating and practicing and he reached enlightenment.

Visualize that Tara's tung shing is standing upright in the middle of the lotus. Recite her ten-syllable mantra, and see that flaming light is coming from her body and the tung shing is emitting a shower of flaming vajras. These destroy all subtle negativities and invisible obstacles. Also think that Tara herself is chanting the syllable HUNG, which frightens off the misleading spirits and destroys their negativities. Under Tara's great protection all realms become calm and peaceful. Generosity, courage, and commitment develop in our hearts so that we become able to fulfill our aspirations to benefit all sentient beings. Then, dissolve the visualization, meditate in the pure nature state, and dedicate the merit.

HIDDEN MEANING

The earth Tara pounds with her feet symbolizes the navel chakra. Earth is the basic element; this whole planet, with its mountains and rivers, is formed from earth. Just so, the navel chakra is the first of the chakras. Our human bodies begin their development from the navel chakra, then the other chakras develop later.

Tara's hands and feet have the two actions of striking and pounding. These two, slapping and stamping, refer to skillful means of practicing on tummo. They also show the movement of the tummo. According to the instructions and one's capability, then the white and red elements are redirected.

In the next line the Praise says, "shattering the seven underworlds." These seven underworlds refer to the movements of the inner fire. In the Kalachakra tantras this is known as Brahma fire, meaning a subtle and refined fire. The Brahma fire is described as like a coiled snake. When the inner heat practice is applied, the refined inner fire spirals upward in seven coils, which are these "seven underworlds." If one is able to guide the inner subtle fire through the seven spirals or coils, it will "shatter" or burn out duality like a brushfire moving through dry grass.

ULTIMATE MEANING

In its pure form the earth symbolizes dharmadhatu, the original nature, or wisdom awareness. The second line points to the two practices of "slapping" and "stamping" needed to actualize this realization. These are none other than the two accumulations of merit and wisdom; according to Dzogchen these are the practices of Trekchö and Tögal. By applying these we remove all the duality and conceptual thought of the seven consciousness states. Ignorance based on the seven states of consciousness is completely dissolved into the totally enlightened state.

15. NOBLE LADY TARA RABZHIMA

*T*ara *Rabzhima's* special activity is purifying our most serious errors and greatest obscurations, so she is called the Tara of purification. *Rabzhima* means "supremely peaceful." Her Praise is:

༄༅།ཕྱག་འཚལ་བདེ་མ་དགེ་མ་ཞི་མ།

(15) CHAG TSHAL DE MA GE MA ZHI MA

Homage, Mother, blissful, virtuous, calm,

༄༅།མྱ་ངན་འདས་ཞི་སྤྱོད་ཡུལ་ཉིད་མ།

NYA NGEN DE ZHI CHÖ YÜL NYI MA

Whose field of activity is peaceful nirvana,

༄༅།སུ་ཧ་ཨོཾ་དང་ཡང་དག་ལྡན་པས།

SO HA OM DANG YANG DAG DEN PE

Endowed with the true perfection of SOHA and OM,

༄༅།སྡིག་པ་ཆེན་པོ་འཇོམས་པ་ཉིད་མ།

DIG PA CHEN PO JOM PA NYI MA

Destroying great evils.

WORD MEANING

Tara Rabzhima's "blissful" state indicates that she is free from suffering and that she gives everyone happiness and frees them from suffering. Looking deeper, what is the cause of happiness? The cause of happiness, joy, and peace is virtue. What is the cause of suffering? Ultimately, the cause of suffering is nonvirtue. Thus the Buddha praises Tara, saying, "Tara, you help all beings now, at the immediate level of the result, and you also help on the ultimate level, the level of the cause. Your field of practice, or *chö yül*, is 'peaceful nirvana,' or immaculate purity and bodhichitta. That is your activity. You are in the state of total calm. You are the embodiment of the dharmakaya, free from obscuration, habitual emotional patterns, grasping, and clinging. Having freed yourself, you are able to free others. Once their obscurations are removed, you bring every being to your state of perfect calm."

There is a beautiful story about Tara's role in the boyhood of one of the great Indian masters, Sthiramati.[87] Actually, the story starts a little before he was born. In his previous life he had been a pigeon, roosting in the rafters of the room used by Master Vasubandhu, the great philosopher.[88] For many years this pigeon listened to Vasubandhu's recitations of the sutras. Then, one day a hawk swooped in through the window and killed the pigeon. Vasubandhu offered many prayers for his "roommate," and the pigeon was reborn as Sthiramati, the son of a wealthy family in southern India. At a young age Sthiramati said, "I must go to find my teacher Vasubandhu," and he set off for central India. When they met, they immediately recognized each other. Sthiramati took monastic vows and went into retreat in a hut with a carved statue of Tara. The little boy believed that she was real. His noon meal was just a handful of chickpeas. Before he began to eat his meal, he made Tara an offering by placing one chickpea on her carved hand. It rolled on the ground. He tried again and again and each chickpea fell into the dust. He was determined not to eat until Tara did! Finally, all the chickpeas were on the ground and the frustrated young boy began to cry, saying, "You're so mean, Tara!" Instantly Tara appeared before him, comforted him, and offered him lots of delicious food. Sthiramati's devotion and wisdom were awakened. He became a great teacher and it is said that Tara always stayed with him thereafter. This story illustrates the power of virtuous action and devotion.

The syllables SOHA[89] and OM will "destroy great evils." This line actually refers to the recitation of the entire ten-syllable mantra, which starts with OM and ends with SOHA. Thus, reciting Tara's mantra will remove all "great evils" and obscurations.

General Meaning

With the supreme bodhichitta motivation, visualize Tara as a rich white color, like the autumn full moon. Her expression is peaceful and smiling. She is holding a blue lotus, and within the center of the lotus there is a slim vase with a narrow neck. The vase is filled with nectar for anointing.[90] While meditating and reciting the mantra, visualize that from Tara Rabzhima and her vase comes light, as well as a rain of purifying water. These completely bathe us and wash away all our greatest errors and emotional obscurations. All beings become completely clean and purified. Thus recite the mantra, dissolve the visualization, meditate on emptiness, and dedicate the merit.

Hidden Meaning

The sequence of four terms, "blissful, virtuous, calm, peaceful nirvana," point out the results of the secret practices on the structure of the vajra body. The tsa, lung, and thigle practices develop one's understanding of the channels and winds, with which one can move the essence elements, or thigle, with the inner heat through the different chakras. With the ascending and descending practices, the four joys, or four great blissfulnesses, arise. So these four qualities, "blissful, virtuous, calm, peaceful nirvana," are the four supremely blissful results of practice with the tsa, lung, thigle, and tummo.

ULTIMATE MEANING

At the Dzogchen level, this is a teaching on the five wisdoms. The phrases "blissful, virtuous, calm, peaceful nirvana" and "destroying great evils" put together refer to these five. They are discriminating awareness wisdom (blissful), mirrorlike wisdom (virtuous), equanimity wisdom (calm), dharmadhatu wisdom (peaceful nirvana), and all-accomplishing wisdom (destroying great evils).

16. Noble Lady Tara
Rigngag Tobjom

The sixteenth emanation of Tara has special abilities to stop the negative intentions of others, such as spells and curses. Her name is *Tara Rigngag Tobjom*. *Rigngag* may have several meanings, but in this case it refers to misusing the mantra or other aspects of practice for evil purposes, to harm. Thus the meaning of her name is "Tara who destroys the power of bad intentions." Her Praise says:

།ཕྱག་འཚལ་ཀུན་ནས་བསྐོར་རབ་དགའ་བའི།

(16) CHAG TSHAL KÜN NE KOR RAB GA WE
Homage, Mother, encompassed by joy,

དགྲ་ཡི་ལུས་ནི་རབ་ཏུ་འགེམས་མ།

DRA YI LÜ NI RAB TU GEM MA
Who shatters the bodies of enemies,

།ཡི་གེ་བཅུ་པའི་ངག་ནི་བཀོད་པའི།

YI GE CHU PE NGAG NI KÖ PE
Savioress manifesting from the rigpa of HUNG,

།རིག་པ་ཧཱུྃ་ལས་སྒྲོལ་མ་ཉིད་མ།

RIG PA HUNG LE DRÖL MA NYI MA
Arraying the sounds of the ten-syllable mantra.

WORD MEANING

The first line speaks of "Mother, encompassed by joy." She is encompassed by her retinue of highly realized beings. These are the great bodhisattvas, arhats, rishis, and vidyadharas. They have attained the highest realization through mantra, meditation, and concentration. They have great samadhi powers and have actualized the different states of the channels, winds, and essences of the subtle body systems.

The second line says, "who shatters the bodies of enemies." The Tibetan verb *gemma* definitely means "shatters" or "smashes." If we drop this (holding up a porcelain vase) on solid rock, I think gemma would be the result.

In this case who are the enemies? The enemies are bad intentions of beings, visible and invisible. These would be intentions to destroy the joy, peace, and benefit of others. Here the language of the Praise is symbolic. It is those intentions, not actual bodies, that Tara is really shattering.

In Buddha's teachings, our human realm is part of the Desire Realm. In another part of the Desire Realm there is a special type of being called a desire god, a kind of greedy and unsatisfied "boss being" who generates or stimulates all kinds of desires. At the end of the recitation of the *Heart Sutra*, there is a section which begins, "Just as, long ago, the king of the gods, Indra, practiced the Prajna-paramita and reversed all the negativities...," followed by three handclaps.[91] The negativities referred to in this chant are what are known as the desires of the gods—desire, attachment, and ego-clinging. These are what King Indra reversed.

Desire develops with sensation and it makes us restless. Among the four maras, or demons, we mentioned before, the Mara of Distraction is actually the same as this desire god. This distraction demon/desire god is a major obstacle to everyone, including Dharma practitioners. This distraction demon arrives in sneaky ways. We may never notice him until it is too late because he appears so attractive and relaxing. But he undermines us. Our strength of realization and practice get separated from our original state or view.

In the context of this Praise, we can understand the desire god as a force that is promoting ego-clinging. Ego-clinging, then, may mislead us into misusing the practice, the mantras, or our meditation power "under the influence" of this desire god. We become wildly intoxicated with our egos and completely lose our mindfulness. Tara Rigngag Tobjom's practice has the power to shatter this intoxication, which is like an evil spell.

"Arraying the sounds of the ten-syllable mantra" shows again the power of Tara's enlightened speech. It is Tara's speech that awakens or empowers the mantra. Think that the ten-syllable mantra of Tara that we all chant is none other than Tara's own voice.

"Savioress manifesting from the rigpa of HUNG" explains what will happen if we continue practicing, meditating, and reciting the ten-syllable mantra. The power of the mantra is such that we will attain the state of Tara, rigpa HUNG, which could be translated as "wisdom awareness HUNG." The mantra will bring us to the totally awakened state, the ultimate state of Tara.

There is another way of understanding this. By continually reciting the ten-syllable mantra with meditation, we will be protected from attempting nonvirtuous activities, such as misusing the spiritual practices in order to hurt. If someone is doing those things to hurt us, by practicing Tara's mantra we are protected in Tara's heart center, in the HUNG state.

GENERAL MEANING

With the correct motivation of bodhichitta, joy, devotion, and appreciation, after doing the "Seven Line Prayer" and lineage prayers, feel the presence of Tara in the pure land of Potala. In the space in front, visualize her as before. Her body is red, and in her left hand she holds a lotus flower with a double vajra (two vajras crossed) at its center.[92] Continually recite the mantra of the ten syllables and feel that masses of wisdom light radiate from the double vajra, as well as from Tara's body. This light completely removes and destroys all the disturbing negativities of speech that come from outside ourselves. Not only that—when the light comes to us and is absorbed, we feel strong peace and joy because the light removes all the obstacles of our interior habitual patterns. All are totally purified into the awakened state. Then the light radiates throughout the whole universe and everything becomes very calm and peaceful. There is no more negative thought, no more negative speech, and no more violence, as every being has now seen the value of love and compassion. In conclusion, we dissolve the visualization, meditate on the true nature, and dedicate the merit.

HIDDEN MEANING

In Vajrayana practice we emphasize purifying the impure winds of our habitual negativities and increasing the wisdom winds within our systems. Yogis and yoginis develop the ability to separate the impure karmic winds from the pure wisdom winds, which are the energies or moving forces of the five wisdoms. "Encompassed by joy" explains the process by which the impure karmic winds are exhaled, while the pure wind is held within and spread through the chakras. "Encompassed" also tells us that there are infinite wisdom airs.

The human body has five basic winds of bodily function, which are the life-sustaining wind, ascending wind, pervasive wind, fire-accompanying wind of digestion, and descending-purgative wind. The five elements, earth, air, fire, water, and space, also have subtle essences, or wind energies. The wind of earth is yellow; of fire, red; of water, white; of air, green; and of space, blue. These ten winds ripen as wisdom, like "the sounds of the ten-syllable mantra."

The second line reads "shatters the bodies of enemies." What are the enemies in the hidden meaning system? The enemies are the mind's dualities, carried on the impure karmic winds, *le lung*. If the pure essence winds are held and spread throughout the system, they will destroy these enemies, duality and the karmic wind systems.

All gross and subtle winds are transformed into the essence of wisdom, which is none other than mantra. Mantra is the movement of awakened energy, which is really the pure wisdom wind. The ultimate state is the inseparability of wisdom wind and mantra, rigpa HUNG.

One dissolves everything within the single state of primordial wisdom, the great bliss-emptiness.

ULTIMATE MEANING

To find the ultimate Dzogchen meaning for "arraying the sounds of the ten-syllable mantra," we look at the Tibetan last line: *rigpa* HUNG *le drölma nyima*. *Rigpa* is awareness, HUNG is the syllable of primordial wisdom, and *drölma nyima* is the original ultimate Tara, all enlightened qualities. Everything is "encompassed by joy" because everything is the display of rigpa. Nothing needs to be rejected, nothing needs to be accepted. Cut through hopes and fears; go beyond borderlines; none of those really exist!

In the enlightened state the notion of "enemies" and of "shattering" are totally transformed. Ego-clinging itself becomes part of the display of rigpa's nature. The identity of this ego-clinging as an "enemy" is thus completely changed and so it is the notion of "enemy" that is "shattered." That is the view of Dzogchen meditation or practice.

At the Dzogchen level the mantra's ten syllables are the ten qualities of enlightenment (five wisdoms and five kayas) and the ten powers of enlightenment.[93] All these are originally inherent in the true nature of reality, the essence of Tara. We discover this as it is.

17 . NOBLE LADY TARA
PAGMÉ NÖNMA

Tara *Pagmé Nönma* protects against obstacles associated with robberies, gangsters, and hunters. She brings beings into a state of calm and tranquility, so she is the Tara of nonviolence. Her name *Pagmé* means "immeasurable, countless" and *Nönma* means "stopping." So this is the Tara who stops countless violent activities. Her Praise is:

།ཕྱག་འཚལ་ཏུ་རེའི་ཞབས་ནི་བརྡབས་པས།

(17) CHAG TSHAL TU RE ZHAB NI DAB PE
Homage, TURE, stamping her feet,

།ཧཱུྃ་གི་རྣམ་པའི་ས་བོན་ཉིད་མ།

HUNG GI NAM PE SA BÖN NYI MA
Whose seed appears in the form of HUNG,

།རི་རབ་མནྡ་ར་དང་འབིགས་བྱེད།

RI RAB MAN DA RA DANG BIG CHE
Shaking Mount Meru, Mandara, Binduchal,

།འཇིག་རྟེན་གསུམ་རྣམས་གཡོ་བ་ཉིད་མ།

JIG TEN SUM NAM YO WA NYI MA
And the triple world.

WORD MEANING

The words of this Praise show the power of Tara's body, speech, and mind to shake the whole universe and bring about peace and nonviolence. That's the simple meaning. In interpreting the names of the mountains, there is some ambiguity. Where the Tibetan says *big che* ['bigs byed] some translators have used the name of Mt. Kailash, which is in Tibet. The Sanskrit word *Kailasha* means snow-capped or glacier mountain. Thus, when Mt. Kailash is used in translating this praise, it is not referring only to that specific holy mountain in Tibet. It stands for all glacier mountains.

However, the literal translation of *big che* is Mt. Binduchal, a renowned holy mountain in India not far from Varanasi. In fact, most of the stones quarried for the buildings of Varanasi came from there. Although Binduchal is described in the texts as very tall, when you go there it doesn't seem very big. It's certainly small compared to the high glacier mountains in Tibet. Maybe it's as high as the Catskill Mountains—maybe not. It's smaller than the famous *Padma Samye Ling* Mountain[94].

In ancient times the Binduchal range was considered the continental divide between north and south India. Buddha visited and gave teachings on this mountain as well as on Vulture's Peak, the King of Mountains. Binduchal is also a holy mountain in Hinduism, a magic or secret place with a lot of traditional stories attached to it. Often in ancient times mountains walked. Once Mt. Binduchal was walking and its movement was crushing lots of sentient beings. Upset at this, Indra threw his vajra and broke Binduchal's feet and legs. Since then, Mt. Binduchal has stopped walking around. Perhaps that's why it is not so tall any more.

So, briefly, Buddha is praising Tara saying, "You who are very strong and powerful, you set trembling all these mighty ones, both sentient beings and nonbeings. You make them humble so they stop all their violent activities, bringing joy and peace to everyone. To you, Tara, I pay homage."

GENERAL MEANING

In visualization we see Tara Pagmé Nönma as orange or golden-red in color, like a beautiful sunrise. Her expression is peaceful but very strong. On her lotus flower she holds a golden stupa.[95] Visualizing this and reciting the ten-syllable mantra, imagine that masses of light in the form of HUNG syllables come in every direction from her body and from the golden stupa. Her power stops violent activities such as robbery and hunting. Everything becomes calm and peaceful. Then dissolve, meditate, and dedicate the merit.

HIDDEN MEANING

The hidden meaning of this Praise to Tara is practice on the three principal channels. According to this system, Mt. Meru or Mt. Sumeru is the central channel, *uma* or avadhuti, while Mt. Mandara and Mt. Binduchal are the right channel, *roma,* and the left channel, *changma.* So when one practices the hidden state of Tara, these three principal channels are filled with the moving essential fluid of the red and white elements.

The fourth line says *jig ten sum nam yo wa nyi ma,* or "shaking the triple world." This is also talking about the three principal channels, but here they are considered in relation to the two wind systems. In both Vajrayana meditation and Tibetan medicine, there are upward, or ascending, winds, and downward, or descending, winds. When the red and white elements fill all the channels, redirected by the upper and lower winds, then there is trembling or moving in different directions. That is what is meant by "shaking the triple world." When one is continually moving, shaking, and expanding the essence elements, the ultimate goal is to merge the white element and red element into the central channel. Then the central channel, the avadhuti, becomes like the blue syllable HUNG, as indicated by the line "whose seed syllable appears in the form of HUNG." If one is able to do that, one goes beyond the conceptual mind state. All conceptions, mundane thoughts, and regular grasping emotions completely disappear.

ULTIMATE MEANING

In the first line, the Dzogchen meaning is pointed out by "TURE." In Sanskrit TURE means swift or quick one, and the Vajrayana or Dzogchen is the quickest path to reach enlightenment. TURE also shows that this path is powerful, energetic, fresh, and full of vitality. There's no way enlightenment will be delayed if we are truly connected with these teachings. How should we start this swift path? We should "stamp with the feet," which means using devotion, bodhichitta, and appreciation. Dzogchen is the highest teaching—there is no question at all about that. However, we need love, devotion, courage, and commitment to travel this path. Our joyful effort is like "feet" we use to realize quickly.

We are instructed to regard our teacher as a buddha. We must also love, appreciate, and honor all great masters, all the teachings, and our own selves. We must recognize this moment as a precious moment. Having those thoughts strongly in our heart, we receive every drop or word of the teachings as precious. This preparation makes practicing Dzogchen quick, swift, and effective: TURE.

The nature of the seed syllable HUNG is none other than rigpa, primordial wisdom. This inherent quality is the ultimate lama: the lamas of the authentic lineages merged into the state of the HUNG syllable. In order to fully receive teaching from a qualified teacher, we must come with devotion and readiness, filled with love and compassion for all living beings. Then we must fully absorb the teaching and use it in a state of joy and appreciation.

When we continue in this practice, every dualistic conception transforms into the three kaya states—dharmakaya, sambhogakaya, and nirmanakaya. "Shaking Mt. Meru" symbolizes shaking our dualistic conceptions or shaking up our habitual patterns of body, speech, and mind. Although right now all of our ego-clinging and neurotic states may look huge and out of reach, like unclimbable mountains, this practice is like an earthquake that shakes them all loose and liberates them into the three kaya states.

18. NOBLE LADY TARA MAJA CHENMO

This Tara's Tibetan name is *Tara Maja Chenmo*. Now *mayura* is the Sanskrit word for "peacock," which is *maja* [rma bya] in Tibetan, so she is the "great one of the peacock." Peacocks are especially associated with protection from poisons because it is said that the peacock eats poison and transforms it into the beauty of its plumage. Thus Tara Maja Chenmo's special activity is counteracting or dispelling inner and outer poisons. These might be from food, water, environmental pollution, or any type of unhealthy situation. Maja Chenmo is also renowned for her compassion in protecting infants and young children.

There's a beautiful traditional story about Tara's role in the great Nagarjuna's[96] childhood. He was born into a rich, high-caste Brahmin family. As was traditional, after his birth the sign-reader came to read the baby's palm. He told Nagarjuna's parents that their son would surely die after one week unless they did certain practices on Tara Maja Chenmo. Although they were Brahmins and didn't want to do this Buddhist practice, they agreed and the threat to Nagarjuna's life was averted for that time.

When he was seven, his parents brought Nagarjuna to Nalanda University. At that time Nalanda was still quite a small university, with only a few temples and buildings. There he received initiation and transmission for the practice of Tara Maja Chenmo, realized it, and it is taught that he extended his life to over six hundred years. The Praise is:

།ཕྱག་འཚལ་ལྷ་ཡི་འཚོ་ཡི་རྣམ་པའི།

(18) CHAG TSHAL LHA YI TSHO YI NAM PE
Homage, Mother holding the rabbit-marked moon,

།རི་དྭགས་རྟགས་ཅན་ཕྱག་ན་བསྣམས་མ།

RI DAG TAG CHEN CHAG NA NAM MA
Which is like a heavenly lake,

།ཏྭ་ར་གཉིས་བརྗོད་ཕཊ་ཀྱི་ཡི་གེས།

TA RA NYI JÖ PHET CHI YI GE
Dispelling all poison with the sound of PHET

།དུག་རྣམས་མ་ལུས་པར་ནི་སེལ་མ།

DUG NAM MA LÜ PAR NI SEL MA
And the twice-spoken TARA.

WORD MEANING

These words portray Tara as totally peaceful and calm by comparing her to a heavenly lake. In the gods' realm there are many remarkable lakes, with totally tranquil water which has great healing energy. That is Tara's state. Like the lake, as soon as we approach her, she will bring us calm. Not only that, but if a ripple of the lake's water (Tara's nature) touches us, it completely cleanses us of all toxic influences.

Tara Maja Chenmo holds the rabbit-marked moon in her hand. In the West people talk of "the man in the moon" because that's how they see the full moon's surface pattern. People in India or Tibet, on the other hand, describe the full moon as either "deer-marked" or "rabbit-marked," *ri dag tag chen.*[97]

In Tibetan medicine there are categories of outer poisons and inner poisons. The outer poisons are subdivided into natural poisons and fabricated poisons, those which are combined or made with an effort. The inner poisons are things that initially seem benign like medicines, but which later become poisonous and can hurt us. Tara protects every living being against all poisons.

GENERAL MEANING

Tara Maja Chenmo is the white color of a glacier mountain touched by the autumn moon. In the middle of the lotus she holds a rabbit-marked full moon. Recite the ten-syllable mantra or the special action mantra.[98] Visualize that beams of white light emanate from her body and the moon she holds, cleansing all our body systems, dispelling all our sicknesses and poisons. She is purifying all other beings and her light cleanses the entire environment of poisons. At the same time Tara's light is giving special protection to all little children. Reciting the mantra, practice in this way, then dissolve the visualization, meditate, and dedicate the merit.

HIDDEN MEANING

Generally, in Vajrayana teaching the moon is a reflection of our inner system, the vajra body. The heavenly lake of the rabbit-marked moon symbolizes our physical vitality and radiance, which depend on the activity of the white thigle. With this practice one "holds," or maintains, the vital white element, expanding it without decreasing so that the lunar white element is like the full moon. So, interiorly, the vitality of the body is developing, just as externally, on a full moon night, the lunar energy is expanding to its peak level. In this practice the vitality develops as the great nondual bliss-emptiness. When it is fully expanded, understanding is complete. It is a sphere, like the moon. Nothing is missing; it doesn't have any flat sides.

When one maintains that full moon energy, one is also able to free oneself from two levels of grasping. This is the liberation attained by the "twice-spoken TARA." One liberates regular grasping and clinging to phenomena and one also liberates spiritual grasping and clinging.

In this case "poison" symbolizes one's obstacles to actualizing the practice of the channels, winds, and essence elements. As one liberates, one simultaneously cuts, or dispels, these poisons with the syllable PHET. Thus one frees oneself from every aspect of these poisons. This summarizes how to practice Tara Maja Chenmo in the system of the vajra structure.

ULTIMATE MEANING

In the Dzogchen teaching Tara's two symbols, the heavenly lake and the rabbit-marked moon, symbolize, respectively, dharmadhatu, the abiding ultimate true nature, and rigpa, the state of innate awareness. There's no division: no dharmadhatu separate from rigpa and no rigpa separate from dharmadhatu. They are united in one single state, the great emptiness-awareness. This is the realization known as "completed like the moon." If we continually apply the two activities of wisdom and skillful means, the "double TARA," and cut with PHET to the state of transparent luminosity, we will quickly attain the enlightened state. We will have transformed all poisons into great healing medicines. There is no longer any conceptual "poison" to be rejected.

19. NOBLE LADY TARA DUGKARMO

Tara *Dugkarmo* is a famous emanation of Tara who protects from nightmares, bad omens in dreams, and black magic. She especially protects the Dharma and the lamas from spiritual harm, as well as protecting us from arguments and violence. *Dugkar* means "white umbrella," so she is often called Queen White Umbrella.[99] Her Praise is:

།ཕྱག་འཚལ་ལྷ་ཡི་ཚོགས་རྣམས་རྒྱལ་པོ།

(19) **CHAG TSHAL LHA YI TSHOG NAM JAL PO**
Homage, Mother served by the ruler of the hosts of gods,

།ལྷ་དང་མི་འམ་ཅི་ཡིས་བསྟེན་མ།

LHA DANG MI AM CHI YI TEN MA
By the gods and kinnaras,

།ཀུན་ནས་གོ་ཆ་དགའ་བས་བརྗིད་ཀྱིས།

KÜN NE GO CHA GA WE JI CHI
Dispelling conflicts and bad dreams

།ཙོད་དང་རྨི་ལམ་ངན་པ་སེལ་མ།

TSÖ DANG MI LAM NGEN PA SEL MA
With her armor of joy and splendor.

WORD MEANING

Buddha's Praise to Tara Dugkarmo teaches that she is the highest of all the mighty ones in our worldly universe, as well as in the worlds of the heavens. She's "served by the ruler," not because she uses her power in a mundane way but because whomever she contacts receives joy and peace. They all serve her, and she maintains peace among them.

The phrase "her armor of joy and splendor" has two symbolic meanings. When we meditate on her, her great peace and joy are like armor which continually protects our own peace and joy. Then, her protection is also armor against bad dreams, curses, disputes, and hostility to the Dharma.

GENERAL MEANING

Tara Dugkarmo is white-colored and her facial expression is passionate—smiling but a little semiwrathful. In the center of her blue lotus flower there is the auspicious symbol of a white umbrella[100] and each of her ornaments symbolizes a virtuous activity. Continually recite Tara's ten-syllable mantra. See that from her body and from the white umbrella sparking light, vajras, and weapons emanate. They come to us and all beings, destroying every obstacle or hindrance. Then visualize that calm and peace arise everywhere. Finally, dissolve the visualization, meditate on the true state of the mind, and dedicate the merit as before.

HIDDEN MEANING

Throughout the Twenty-one Praises, the hidden meanings are related to the vajra body. Thus, at this level "ruler of the gods" refers to the central channel, or uma. The "gods and kinnaras" are the two side channels. "Her armor of joy and splendor" is a means of giving instructions on how to apply and maintain the great bliss developed through the practice of moving the red and white elements. "Armor" indicates maintaining and protecting the bliss by concealing the elements.

There are four different armors or concealments. First, all the channels are concealed within the central channel. Second, all the winds are concealed within the indestructible wisdom wind system. Third, the thigle, or essence element, is hidden or kept in the emptiness state. Fourth, emptiness is kept in the primordial wisdom state, in the dharmadhatu of great bliss-emptiness. Those are the four different ways of concealment or armor.

If one is able to do that practice, all blockages will be released. Then the notion of samsara and one's habitual patterns cannot destroy what one has developed and realized. That is the result described as "dispelling conflicts and bad dreams."

ULTIMATE MEANING

The "ruler of hosts" is none other than rigpa, the naked true awareness that we discover upon its being introduced to us by the qualified teacher or lineage master. If we maintain that view, we will also increase and complete the two accumulation practices of wisdom and merit, symbolized by gods and kinnaras. All perceptions related to the six consciousnesses, and all notions of samsara, are liberated into the wisdom state. Worries, hesitations, and doubts all disappear. Nothing is disturbing. There is nothing to be rejected or accepted. Everything becomes magnificent joy. This joyous wisdom is our "armor." That is the ultimate way of "dispelling conflict and bad dreams."

20. NOBLE LADY TARA
RITÖ LOMA JÖNMA

Tara *Ritö Loma Jönma* is known for giving protection against contagious diseases, plagues, and fevers. Roughly translated, *Ritö* means "mountain hermitage," *Loma* means "leaves of a tree," and *Jönma* means "wearing." So this is the Tara wearing the leaves of a tree in her mountain retreat. In many of the traditional stories about Tara, she appears as a lady dressed in leaves to save a devotee from a fearful situation. Her Praise says:

།ཕྱག་འཚལ་ཉི་མ་ཟླ་བ་རྒྱས་པའི།

(20) CHAG TSHAL NYI MA DA WA JE PE
Homage, Mother, whose two eyes

སྤྱན་གཉིས་པོ་ལས་འོད་རབ་གསལ་མ།

CHEN NYI PO LE Ö RAB SAL MA
Are the sun and full moon, shining with brilliant light,

།ཧ་ར་གཉིས་བརྗོད་ཏུཏྟཱ་ར་ཡིས།

HA RA NYI JÖ TUT TA RA YI
Who dispels deadly disease

།ཤིན་ཏུ་དྲག་པོའི་རིམས་ནད་སེལ་མ།

SHIN TU DRAG PÖ RIM NE SEL MA
With TUTTARA and twice-spoken HARA.

WORD MEANING

The word meaning of this Praise by the Buddha says, "Your eyes, Tara Ritö Loma Jönma, have the energy of the sun and moon. Your right eye, like the sun, has the power to destroy sickness[101] and your left eye, like the moon, has the power to bring back health. When one recites your mantra with TUTTARA and the double HARA, you will dispel deadly contagious diseases and sicknesses."

GENERAL MEANING

We visualize Tara Ritö Loma Jönma in a golden-red or saffron color with the usual posture and mudras. She is holding a blue lotus flower on which is a *za ma tog*, a container full of medicinal substances. We can recite the ten-syllable mantra or the action mantra.[102] Visualize receiving lots of light from Tara and from the container, dispelling all sicknesses and bringing both external and internal health. With this thought meditate on Tara, dissolve the visualization, meditate on the true nature, and dedicate the merit.

HIDDEN MEANING

As before, sun and moon symbolize the red element and the white element, respectively. The two eyes correspond to the two syllables which reside at the ends of the central channel, the inverted HANG at the crown chakra and the short A below the navel chakra. "Brilliant light" is the clear light which arises from practicing with the channels. The double HARA symbolizes the two stages, visualization stage and completion, or dissolving, stage. HARA is a Sanskrit word which can mean both "to take away" with a forceful sense, like stealing, or "to take in." Therefore, HARA has a double meaning; when something is taken away, something is also gained. With these practices one takes oneself away from samsara and nirvana. Simultaneously, one gains actualization of the great union of bliss-emptiness.

TUTTARA has the meaning of fiery, passionate longing or yearning. The practitioner understands the meaning of the sun and moon energy and actualizes great warmth, which will destroy all sickness. Contagious diseases and all obstacles will be dispelled.

ULTIMATE MEANING

At the ultimate level of reality, the sun and moon symbolize the two qualities of the original Great Perfection, ka dak, meaning "primordially pure," and lhün drub, meaning "spontaneously self-perfected." Tara's two eyes show two methods of application, symbolizing practical instructions on Trekchö and Tögal. When these inner systems of Trekchö and Tögal are mastered, all habitual patterns will be released and many enlightened qualities will arise as "brilliant light." The "twice-spoken HARA" is waking ourselves up from the illusory world of our ordinary delusions. Dualities disappear, as if we were waking up from a dreadful dream. All the feverish, deluded projections of our imaginations just dissolve like a nightmare.

21. NOBLE LADY TARA
LHAMO ÖZER CHENMA

*T*ara *Lhamo Özer Chenma* is the divine great Mother of "brilliant light rays," *Özer*. She is particularly beneficial to us because she can protect our longevity. She helps us when our energy, vitality, or life force is endangered. She is also renowned as the protectress of animals. Her Praise reads:

ཕྱག་འཚལ་དེ་ཉིད་གསུམ་རྣམས་བཀོད་པས།

(21) CHAG TSHAL DE NYI SUM NAM KÖ PE

Homage, Mother, endowed with the power to pacify

ཞི་བའི་མཐུ་དང་ཡང་དག་ལྡན་མ།

ZHI WE THU DANG YANG DAG DEN MA

By the array of the three natural states,

གདོན་དང་རོ་ལངས་གནོད་སྦྱིན་ཚོགས་རྣམས།

DÖN DANG RO LANG NÖ JIN TSOG NAM

Destroying the hosts of evil spirits, yakshas, and the walking dead,

འཇོམས་པ་ཏུ་རེ་རབ་མཆོག་ཉིད་མ།

JOM PA TU RE RAB CHOG NYI MA

TURE, most excellent Mother.

WORD MEANING

This Praise shows that Tara's natural body, speech, and mind are none other than the vajra body, vajra speech, and vajra mind of the buddhas. The three syllables OM, AH, and HUNG, symbolizing the three vajra states, are completely her nature, as it is. So Buddha is saying, "Tara, you are in the three vajra states; you bring everyone into that condition and you protect everyone from obstacles within the three vajra states. You have supreme pacifying power and you lead everyone with your power. To you, Mother Tara, I pay homage."

Tibetan medicine and other teachings contain long lists of obstacles to health and longevity. There are eighteen different types of *dön*, or evil influences. Yakshas, or *nöjin* in Tibetan, means "harm-givers." They are demons which steal the vitality or radiance of humans. Vetalas, or *rolangs* in Tibetan, are the "walking dead," or zombies. They are associated with using mantra in the wrong way, using dead bodies to carry out harmful actions, and being able to change their forms. All of these forces can be counteracted through practicing with the power to pacify with which Tara Lhamo Özer Chenma is endowed.

GENERAL MEANING

Visualize that Lhamo Özer Chenma's color is a very rich white. In her hand she holds a blue lotus, upon which stands a golden fish.[103] Continually reciting the ten-syllable mantra, see that from Tara and from the golden fish wisdom light emanates out and summons back to us and all beings all the vitality and energies which have been lost. We acquire more inner radiance and become more bright and clear. All sick animals are also benefited. All beings become calm and peaceful in their own way and none are disturbed or violent. To conclude the practice, dissolve, meditate, and dedicate the merit from this practice on Lhamo Özer Chenma.

HIDDEN MEANING

The hidden meanings of this Praise to Lhamo Özer Chenma are instructions on the experiences of death. The Tibetan phrase *de nyi sum* is translated here as "the three natural states."

The body is composed of six elements. As death approaches, these elements decrease. When we die, it is said that the three natural states of abiding will come, one after another. These occur during the first bardo[104] state, the *chö nyi bardo*, or bardo of the true nature. The beginning of the chö nyi bardo is marked by the departure of the bodhichitta elements from their original physical locations. During ordinary life, as we know, the white element resides on the crown chakra and the red element resides below the navel center. As death approaches, the white and red elements leave their positions and move toward the heart center. Three different experiences, related to the three states of abiding, arise very briefly. The first experience is an experience of appearance or clarity; it is like the light of a full moon shining through a skylight, occurring as the white element melts into the heart center. Then follows the increase, or bliss experience, of flashing red light like a burning fire as the red element melts into the heart. As the two elements merge, the consciousness is held and everything becomes dark and motionless for a time, in the attainment or no-thought state. These three, then, are the de nyi sum or "three states of abiding." Next, after that motionless state, the *ö sal* (or clear light luminosity state) arises.

The "power to pacify" is this clear light luminosity state, or Mother clear light. It appears for an extremely short time, but one experiences it. However, one may not recognize the experience.

The dön symbolize the channels (tsa), the nöjin symbolize the karmic winds (lung) and conceptual thought, and the rolangs symbolize the essences (thigle). When one recognizes and maintains the clear light luminosity state of the "triple suchness" (another way of translating the Tibetan phrase *de nyid sum*), at that moment the notions of tsa, lung, and thigle, as well as concepts of errors and mistakes in the practice, dissolve, and all of that business is finished. One reaches the ultimate calm peaceful state.

TURE means "quick one." At the moment when the Mother clear light appears, if one recognizes it, one has the opportunity to reach enlightenment instantly. Therefore, here is the direct route to enlightenment, the quickest way.

ULTIMATE MEANING

These "three natural states" at the ultimate level are the true nature of the cause, result, and essence. So it is said that the cause is beyond characteristics, the result is beyond expectation, and the essence of both cause and result is the total emptiness of self-awareness wisdom, rigpa. Rigpa has the three characteristics of emptiness, clarity, and unceasing energy. The emptiness aspect of rigpa is dharmakaya, the clarity (or brightness aspect) of rigpa is sambhogakaya, and the unceasing compassionate energy of rigpa is nirmanakaya.

Tara has the "endowment" of these three natural states. We could use the word "settling" for her condition of endowment. When we recognize this rigpa and relax or settle into it, we instantly just settle in the dharmakaya state. We don't have to move anywhere and we don't have to transfer ourselves from one state to another. All dualistic conceptions dissolve, or self-liberate, just as ice melts into water. The chunks of ice are our habitual patterns and all those yakshas, döns, or rolangs are our dualistic creations. Now, all that melts into the original state and we reach enlightenment in the embodiment of the three kayas. This is the supreme realization, the quick realization, and the highest teaching.

We practitioners are fortunate to have become connected to the Dzogchen teachings; we don't have to wait a long time to reach the enlightened state. It may only take a moment—TURE. If we become realized in the morning, we reach enlightenment in the morning—before breakfast, even! If we realize after lunch, we reach enlightenment that same afternoon. If we attain realization after tea, then we will be enlightened even before dinner.[105] So we can make a celebration at any time of the day: breakfast is a celebration for the enlightenment of the morning-enlightened beings, lunch is the celebration for the afternoon-enlightened ones, and so forth. For a fortunate and capable person, there's not too much effort; merely by connecting with one's rigpa, he or she will wake up.

That's it!

PART FOUR

Verses on the Benefits
Concise Summary

ༀ། །རྩ་བའི་སྔགས་ཀྱི་བསྟོད་པ་འདི་དང་།

TSA WAI NGAG CHI TÖ PA DI DANG

This is the praise with the root mantra,

།ཕྱག་འཚལ་བ་ནི་ཉི་ཤུ་རྩ་གཅིག།

CHAG TSHAL WA NI NYI SHU TSA CHIG

And these are the twenty-one homages.

།ལྷ་མོ་ལ་གུས་ཡང་དག་ལྡན་པའི།

LHA MO LA GÜ YANG DAG DEN PE

Reverently recited by whoever has intelligence

།བློ་ལྡན་གང་གིས་རབ་དད་བརྗོད་དེ།

LO DEN GANG GI RAB DE JÖ DE

And genuine devotion to the goddess,

།སྲོད་དང་ཐོ་རངས་ལངས་པར་བྱས་ནས།

SÖ DANG THO RANG LANG PAR JE NE

Arising at dawn or evening to remember it,

།དྲན་པས་མི་འཇིགས་ཐམས་ཅད་རབ་སྟེར།

DREN PE MI JIG THAM CHE RAB TER

It grants complete fearlessness.

ཕྱིག་པ་ཐམས་ཅད་རབ་ཏུ་ཞི་བྱེད།

DIG PA THAM CHE RAB TU ZHI JE
All evil deeds are pacified;

ངན་འགྲོ་ཐམས་ཅད་འཇོམས་པ་ཉིད་དོ།

NGEN DRO THAM CHE JOM PA NYI DO
All evil destinies are destroyed.

རྒྱལ་བ་བྱེ་བ་ཕྲག་བདུན་རྣམས་ཀྱིས།

JAL WA JE WA TRAG DÜN NAM CHI
Quickly, one will be initiated

མྱུར་དུ་དབང་ནི་བསྐུར་བར་འགྱུར་ལ།

NYUR DU WANG NI KUR WAR JUR LA
By the seventy million buddhas.

འདི་ལས་ཆེ་བ་ཉིད་ནི་འཐོབ་ཅིང་།

DI LE CHE WA NYI NI THOB CHING
Attaining greatness by this practice,

སངས་རྒྱས་གོ་འཕང་མཐར་ཐུག་དེར་འགྲོ།

SANG JE GO PHANG THAR THUG DER DRO
One will proceed to the ultimate state, buddhahood.

དེ་ཡིས་དུག་ནི་དྲག་པོ་ཆེན་པོ།

DE YI DUG NI DRAG PO CHEN PO
Even if one has eaten or drunk

།བཏུན་གནས་པའམ་གཞན་ཡང་འགྲོ་བ།

TEN NE PA AM ZHEN YANG DRO WA

A dreadful poison, vegetable or animal,

།ཟོས་པ་དང་ནི་འཐུང་པ་ཉིད་ཀྱང་།

ZÖ PA DANG NI THUNG PA NYI CHANG

By remembering the praise, the poison is completely dispelled.

།དྲན་པས་རབ་ཏུ་སེལ་བ་ཉིད་འཐོབ།

DREN PE RAB TU SEL WA NYI THOB

One completely abandons the hosts of sufferings

།གདོན་དང་རིམས་དང་དུག་གིས་གཟིར་བའི།

DÖN DANG RIM DANG DUG GI ZIR WE

Caused by evil spirits,

།སྡུག་བསྔལ་ཚོགས་ནི་རྣམ་པར་སྤངས་ཏེ།

DUG NGAL TSHOG NI NAM PAR PANG TE

Contagious diseases and poisons,

།སེམས་ཅན་གཞན་པ་རྣམས་ལ་ཡང་ངོ་།

SEM CHEN ZHEN PA NAM LA YANG NGO

For other beings as well.

།གཉིས་གསུམ་བདུན་དུ་མངོན་པར་བརྗོད་ན།

NYI SUM DÜN DU NGÖN PAR JÖ NA

If one recites the praise clearly two, three, or seven times,

ཁྱུ་འདོད་པས་ནི་བུ་ཐོབ་གྱུར་ཞིང་།

BU DÖ PE NI BU THOB JUR ZHING

Those wishing for sons will gain sons.

ཁྱོར་འདོད་པས་ནི་ནོར་རྣམས་ཉིད་ཐོབ།

NOR DÖ PE NI NOR NAM NYI THOB

Those wishing for wealth will gain wealth.

འདོད་པ་ཐམས་ཅད་ཐོབ་པར་འགྱུར་ལ།

DÖ PA THAM CHE THOB PAR JUR LA

All desires will be fulfilled.

བགེགས་རྣམས་མེད་ཅིང་སོ་སོ་འཇོམས་འགྱུར།

GEG NAM ME CHING SO SO JOM JUR

There will be no hindrances, all obstacles will be destroyed.

An intelligent one[106] who is devoted to the Divine Lady will recite these twenty-one verses of praise to the Noble Lady Tara's emanations with strong devotion and thinking of all sentient beings. Whether you do this practice in the morning or evenings, if done with a clear mind, it will remove all obstacles and fears. Even thinking of Tara will bring total calm, peace, and protection from all fears and all frightening situations. Tara's practice removes the two obscurations: negative emotions and subtle conceptual thinking. It will increase the two merits: accumulation merit and wisdom merit. From the moment you start praying to and practicing Tara, your life will be always under the protection of the Great Mother. From then on rebirth in the lower realms will be prevented. If you do this prayer for others, it will bring them the same benefits; it will protect them in their lifetimes as well as uproot future births in the lower realms. So there is great benefit.

Noble Lady Tara is the Mother of all the buddhas of the past, present, and future, as well as all the bodhisattvas and all the enlightened ones. Therefore, when you practice Tara, all the numberless buddhas and enlightened beings always bless you, empower you, and protect you. There is no greater benefit or accomplishment to be obtained than that of practicing Tara. It is also true that when you practice Tara you are on a "one way street" to buddhahood. There will be no U-turns and no detours; you are certain to move forward to enlightenment.

Practicing Tara will also transcend all bad circumstances. Poisons can be transformed into medicines by meditating on her. Therefore, she is a great healer. By transcending or transmuting all the bad circumstances, negativities, contagious diseases, and poisons into a beautiful state, you will remove all the troubles that need Tara's benefits. All suffering and difficulties are removed by chanting these beautiful verses. They are for you; they are for all beings.

Devoted practitioners, chant these prayers two times, three times, seven times or as many as you have time. More is better. Our final goal is to reach buddhahood and to remove *all* suffering and difficulties, ignorance and attachment. Until we reach that goal we should not stop at small-scale benefits and be satisfied with little. Don't forget your goal, but continue to practice until you fulfill all wishes.

If lay practitioners want a son, they will have a son. Or if they want a girl, they will have a girl. Those who prefer the temporary benefit of wealth can become wealthy. Tara's Praises will secure all worldly wishes, as well as fulfill the special wishes of bodhichitta. Every obstacle will be removed, every suffering soothed, and every achievement will become a beautiful gift. That is the brief meaning of these verses of the Buddha Shakyamuni explaining the benefits of the prayers.

This teaching has been a detailed exploration of the twenty-one emanations of Tara, according to four levels of teaching and meaning. However, we reiterate that reading and receiving this as "information" is not by itself sufficient. Everything is brought to fruition through practice. Whatever life experiences we have, we can practice with them by connecting to Tara with our meditation.

Our Tara practice needs to be simple, meaningful, and accurate. So that no mistakes happen, we will stress once more the crucial three supreme practices, the very foundation of meaningful activity. While we call this the foundation, it is in a way both the take-off place and the landing place for our enlightenment. Without this foundation, at best our practice is unlikely to achieve much; at worst our delusions will wreck our practice.

The first supreme practice is the noble motivation of refuge, bodhichitta, and devotion. Refuge is the feeling of closeness and warmth towards the Three Jewels and the full appreciation of our own true nature. Bodhichitta is the thought of love and compassion for all living beings without any exceptions. The method or application for bodhichitta is engaging in the four boundless practices of boundless love, compassion, joy, and equanimity.

Our method for developing these from the heart is to say these universal words of the Buddha and ancient great masters:

།སེམས་ཅན་ཐམས་ཅད་བདེ་བ་དང་བདེ་བའི་རྒྱུ་དང་ལྡན་པར་གྱུར་ཅིག

**SEM CHEN THAM CHE DE WA DANG DE WE JU DANG
DEN PAR JUR CHIG**

May all beings have happiness and the cause of happiness.

།སྡུག་བསྔལ་དང་སྡུག་བསྔལ་གྱི་རྒྱུ་དང་བྲལ་བར་གྱུར་ཅིག

**DUG NGAL DANG DUG NGAL JI JU DANG DREL WAR
JUR CHIG**

May they be free from suffering and the cause of suffering.

།སྡུག་བསྔལ་མེད་པའི་བདེ་བ་དམ་པ་དང་མི་འབྲལ་བར་གྱུར་ཅིག

**DUG NGAL ME PE DE WA DAM PA DANG MI DRAL
WAR JUR CHIG**

May they never be dissociated from the supreme happiness which is
without suffering.

ཉེ་རིང་ཆགས་སྡང་གཉིས་དང་བྲལ་བའི་བཏང་སྙོམས་ཚད་མེད་པ་ལ་
གནས་པར་གྱུར་ཅིག།

**NYE RING CHAG DANG NYI DANG DRAL WE TANG
NYOM TSHE ME PA LA NE PAR JUR CHIG**

May they remain in boundless equanimity, free from both attachment to close ones and rejection of others.

When chanting this, we try to really connect with what we are
chanting and feel its meaning in the marrow of our bones, coming back
to the true compassion and wisdom of our hearts and minds.

Devotion creates readiness, just as in the spring the sun and rain make gardens ready to plant seeds and start growth. Devotion is the key that opens the door of pure vision. It leads us beyond darkness, doubt, and hesitation; it will help us recover from periods of difficulty. Devotion takes us beyond conceptions to an understanding of the true nature.

The second supreme practice is maintaining a particular state of mind during the practice itself. We aspire to a nonconceptually performed practice, free from grasping or clinging. What does this mean? It means that when we practice or meditate, we should not relate to our visualization as if it were our creation, or as if it were a solid object. These errors would simply form more mental conceptions to trap us. Our visualization must be experienced as a dynamic display of the true nature, like the transcendental wisdom rainbow body. We must understand that the visualization is totally empty of inherent existence, yet totally full of dynamic energies of love, compassion, and wisdom. In this case this dynamic display of the true nature appears in the form of the Buddha Tara.

We have described many different ways to practice Tara. If we have the capacity to do the practice of these twenty-one emanations every day, step-by-step, one after another, that is great. But it is also fine to practice a single Tara, bringing all the qualities and activities of Tara into one emanation and working with just one level of practice. A single Tara can lead us to enlightenment.

We all have difficulties with clear visualization. That is nothing unusual; we *all* have that. Don't become discouraged! During the visualization the most important thing is to feel Tara's presence and to maintain our foundation, which is the motivation of closeness and loving-kindness directed to all living beings. When we apply that motivation, even if our visualization doesn't develop as exactly as the text says, or as clearly as we hope, the practice is going to work. What does that mean? It means that our practice is going to generate the benefits that are promised and that we will receive Tara's blessings and realizations. If we have a firm foundation as our "take-off place" and recite the ten-syllable mantra without becoming discouraged, have confidence that the visualization will develop more clearly later on.

Green Tara is the source of the other emanations of Tara. Most of the time we focus our practice on Green Tara. If we wish to practice other Taras, such as Red Tara, White Tara, or Blue-black Tara, their gestures, postures, and costumes are the same. What differs are the body colors, facial expressions, hand objects, the energies emitted by that emanation of Tara, whether lights, sounds, flaming vajras, and so forth, and the purpose or effects of these energies.

When we practice on the Twenty-one Emanations of Tara, we may place any of the Taras in the center of our visualization. In some sadhanas we self-visualize as Tara, or as Yeshe Tsogyal or other wisdom dakinis. Mostly, though, it is suggested to visualize Tara right in front of oneself in space. For example, if we practice on Red Tara, then we visualize Red Tara directly before us. She will be surrounded by the other twenty Taras, together with all the buddhas and bodhisattvas. If it's a little too "crowded" to visualize all twenty-one deities at once, just do the central figure. View her as the embodiment of all the Taras of the dharmakaya, sambhogakaya, and nirmanakaya, as well as all the other buddhas and bodhisattvas. In that way every enlightened being is within her. So to summarize, the instruction is to practice every Tara the same way, varying only the color, hand object, and the activity that radiates from Tara's form and from her hand object.

When we practice Tara, it's not necessary to do all four levels. We can simply practice the general meaning, reciting the mantra, and the ultimate meaning, the Dzogchen method. That will be really great! First we practice the general meaning, the visualization (or creation) stage. We follow that with the completion (or dissolving) stage. Dissolved means just that—dissolved, not destroyed or finished.

When we dissolve, what happens? We enter a state of fullness where there is no separation, no break or gap. Tara is no longer just a limited visualized image of Tara; she becomes the pervasive Tara nature, subtle and profound, beyond any limitation, naturally embracing everything. When we dissolve, we connect to this without any effort. We embrace that reality without any separation. This is the ultimate state of Tara practice and it is important to maintain our awareness in that state beyond mental focus as long as we have time. Because Dzogchen is beyond focus, conceptions, and effort, this is none other than the ultimate state of Dzogchen.

We have two different sadhanas available for practicing on Tara. *The Daily Recitation of Revered Noble Tara*, or *Je tsün dröl me jün cher ni*, was written by His Holiness Düdjom Rinpoche. It is a complete sadhana practice which incorporates the Twenty-one Praises to Tara. If we have less time, we can do a part of it by chanting the Praises with the visualization of Tara, reciting the mantra for as long as we have time, and then dissolving, meditating, and dedicating the merit. Generally it is always good to chant the Twenty-one Praises. The whole text is a powerful mantra and very blissful to chant. It is really the word of the Buddha.

If we have very little time, we can chant the short Green Tara prayer of two stanzas found in *The Blessing Treasure: A Liturgy of the Buddha* (*Tub chog jin lab ter dzö zhug so*). This prayer is from very famous ancient Indian masters.

om   po ta la yi gnas mchog nas
OM   PO TA LA YI NE CHOG NE
OM   In the pure land of Potala,

ཏཾ་ཡིག་ལྗང་ཁུ་ལས་འཁྲུངས་ཤིང་།

tam yig ljang khu las 'khrungs shing
TAM YIG JANG KHU LE THRUNG SHING
You who emanated from the green TAM syllable,

ཏྃ་ཡིག་འོད་ཀྱིས་འགྲོ་བ་སྒྲོལ།

tam yig 'od kyis 'gro ba sgrol

TAM YIG Ö CHI DRO WA DRÖL

Liberating sentient beings by the light of the TAM syllable,

སྒྲོལ་མ་འཁོར་བཅས་གཤེགས་སུ་གསོལ།

sgrol ma 'khor bcas gshegs su gsol

DRÖL MA KHOR CHE SHEG SU SÖL

Please approach, noble Tara, with your retinue.

ལྷ་དང་ལྷ་མིན་ཅོད་པན་གྱིས།

lha dang lha min cod pan gyis

LHA DANG LHA MIN CHÖ PEN JI

The jeweled crowns of the gods and asuras

ཞབས་ཀྱི་པདྨོ་ལ་བཏུད་ཅིང་།

zhabs kyi padmo la btud cing

ZHAB CHI PEMO LA TÜ CHING

Bow down to your lotus feet.

ཕོངས་པ་ཀུན་ལས་སྒྲོལ་མཛད་མ།

phongs pa kun las sgrol mdzad ma

PHONG PA KÜN LE DRÖL DZE MA

You who free all beings from trouble and misfortune,

སྒྲོལ་མ་ཡུམ་ལ་ཕྱག་འཚལ་བསྟོད།

sgrol ma yum la phyag 'tshal bstod

DRÖL MA YUM LA CHAG TSHAL TÖ

To you I prostrate, Mother Tara.

Next say one mala of Tara's mantra:

ༀ་ཏུ་རེ་ཏུཏྟ་རེ་ཏུ་རེ་སྭ་ཧཱ།

OM TARE TUTTARE TURE SOHA

or as much as you are able. Continue with the prayer revealed by
the great tertön Düdjom Lingpa, predecessor of His Holiness Düdjom Rinpoche:

རྗེ་བཙུན་འཕགས་མ་སྒྲོལ་མ་ཁྱེད་མཁྱེན་ནོ།

rje btsun 'phags ma sgrol ma khyed mkhyen no
JE TSÜN PHAG MA DRÖL MA CHE CHEN NO
Noble Lady Tara, please watch over us.

འཇིགས་དང་སྡུག་བསྔལ་ཀུན་ལས་བསྐྱབ་ཏུ་གསོལ།

'jigs dang sdug bsngal kun las bskyab tu gsol
JIG DANG DUG NGAL KÜN LE CHAB TU SÖL
Protect us from all suffering and fear.

Chant that three times or seven times, and then meditate. That is
the shortest, simplest way of all to do practice on Tara.

Finally, we should conclude every practice, no matter how short,
with the third supreme practice, the dedication of merit. When we
dedicate, we multiply and share the merit. Because we began our
practice with the intention to benefit all living beings and continued it with that view, whatever merit, spiritual energy, or realization
we obtain we share at the end with all beings without exception.
Use the prayer in *A Small Treasury of Prayers of Supplication and Dedication* (*Söl deb dang ngo mön nyung du zhug so*). If these aren't available, use some of the many other prayers of dedication available,
written by the great masters.

With dedication we also include aspiration prayers. Aspirations are sources of courage and commitment. They restrengthen our bodhichitta and confidence, which increases our capabilities. Make dedication and aspiration prayers at the end of every session of practice, as well as every time we complete some helpful work for ourselves, another person, or other beings in general.

Noble Lady Tara is the true embodiment of all the buddhas and bodhisattvas, arhats, and realized beings. Tara is also the true embodiment of all the lineage masters who shared their realizations, thereby continually inspiring and sparking students to the enlightened state. When we practice Tara, we connect our minds to every one of these great ones. We receive their blessings, energy, love, compassion, courage, and commitment for our path to realization for the benefit of other beings.

In essence, what actually is Tara? She is primordial wisdom, the Source, the true Mother of all phenomena. All the appearances of samsara and nirvana arise as the display of wisdom dakini Tara. Tara embodies all possible aspects of the enlightened nature, the totally awakened state. To Buddha Tara we pay spontaneous, joyous homage.

The Twenty-one
Praises to Tara

།ཨོཾ་རྗེ་བཙུན་མ་འཕགས་མ་སྒྲོལ་མ་ལ་ཕྱག་འཚལ་ལོ།

om rje btsun ma 'phags ma sgrol ma la phyag 'tshal lo

OM JE TSÜN MA PHAG MA DRÖL MA LA CHAG TSHAL LO

OM Homage to Noble Lady Tara.

།ཕྱག་འཚལ་ཏ་རེ་མྱུར་མ་དཔའ་མོ།

phyag 'tshal ta re myur ma dpa' mo

CHAG TSHAL TA RE NYUR MA PA MO

Homage to Tara, quick one, heroine.

།ཏུཏྟ་ར་ཡིས་འཇིགས་པ་སེལ་མ།

tutta ra yis 'jigs pa sel ma

TU TA RA YI JIG PA SEL MA

With TUTTARA, you are the one who banishes all fear.

།ཏུ་རེས་དོན་ཀུན་སྦྱིན་པས་སྒྲོལ་མ།

tu res don kun sbyin pas sgrol ma

TU RE DÖN KÜN JIN PE DRÖL MA

With TURE, the liberator who bestows all benefits.

།སྭ་ཧཱའི་ཡི་གེས་ཁྱོད་ལ་འདུད་དོ།

sva ha'i yi ges khyod la 'dud do

SO HE YI GE CHÖ LA DÜ DO

With SOHA, I pay homage to you.

ཕྱག་འཚལ་སྒྲོལ་མ་མྱུར་མ་དཔའ་མོ།

phyag 'tshal sgrol ma myur ma dpa' mo

(1) CHAG TSHAL DRÖL MA NYUR MA PA MO

Homage, Tara, quick one,

སྤྱན་ནི་སྐད་ཅིག་གློག་དང་འདྲ་མ།

spyan ni skad cig glog dang 'dra ma

CHEN NI KE CHIG LOG DANG DRA MA

Heroine whose eyes flash like lightning.

འཇིག་རྟེན་གསུམ་མགོན་ཆུ་སྐྱེས་ཞལ་གྱི།

'jig rten gsum mgon chu skyes zhal gyi

JIG TEN SUM GÖN CHU CHE ZHAL JI

Born from the opening corolla of the lotus face

གེ་སར་བྱེ་བ་ལས་ནི་བྱུང་མ།

ge sar bye ba las ni byung ma

GE SAR JE WA LE NI JUNG MA

Of the lord of the triple world.

།ཕྱག་འཚལ་སྟོན་ཀའི་ཟླ་བ་ཀུན་ཏུ།

phyag 'tshal ston ka'i zla ba kun tu

(2) CHAG TSHAL TÖN KE DA WA KÜN TU

Homage, Mother whose face is filled

།གང་བ་བརྒྱ་ནི་བརྩེགས་པའི་ཞལ་མ།

gang ba brgya ni brtsegs pa'i zhal ma

GANG WA JA NI TSEG PE ZHAL MA

With the light of an array of a hundred full autumn moons,

།སྐར་མ་སྟོང་ཕྲག་ཚོགས་པ་རྣམས་ཀྱིས།

skar ma stong phrag tshogs pa rnams kyis

KAR MA TONG THRAG TSHOG PA NAM CHI

Shining with the brilliant open light

།རབ་ཏུ་ཕྱེ་བའི་འོད་རབ་འབར་མ།

rab tu phye ba'i 'od rab 'bar ma

RAB TU CHE WE Ö RAB BAR MA

Of the hosts of a thousand stars.

།ཕྱག་འཚལ་སེར་སྔོ་ཆུ་ནས་སྐྱེས་ཀྱིས།

phyag 'tshal ser sngo chu nas skyes kyis
(3) **CHAG TSHAL SER NGO CHU NE CHE CHI**
Homage, Mother, golden one,

།པདྨས་ཕྱག་ནི་རྣམ་པར་བརྒྱན་མ།

padmas phyag ni rnam par brgyan ma
PE ME CHAG NI NAM PAR JEN MA
Her hand adorned with a blue lotus,

།སྦྱིན་པ་བརྩོན་འགྲུས་དཀའ་ཐུབ་ཞི་བ།

sbyin pa brtson 'grus dka' thub zhi ba
JIN PA TSÖN DRÜ KA THUB ZHI WA
Whose field of practice is generosity, effort,

།བཟོད་པ་བསམ་གཏན་སྤྱོད་ཡུལ་ཉིད་མ།

bzod pa bsam gtan spyod yul nyid ma
ZÖ PA SAM TEN CHÖ YÜL NYI MA
Austerity, calm, acceptance, and meditation.

།ཕྱག་འཚལ་དེ་བཞིན་གཤེགས་པའི་གཙུག་ཏོར།

phyag 'tshal de bzhin gshegs pa'i gtsug tor
(4) **CHAG TSHAL DE ZHIN SHEG PE TSUG TOR**
Homage, Crown of Tathagata,

།མཐའ་ཡས་རྣམ་པར་རྒྱལ་བ་སྤྱོད་མ།

mtha' yas rnam par rgyal ba spyod ma
THA YE NAM PAR JAL WA CHÖ MA
Her actions endlessly victorious,

།མ་ལུས་ཕ་རོལ་ཕྱིན་པ་ཐོབ་པའི།

ma lus pha rol phyin pa thob pa'i
MA LÜ PHA RÖL CHIN PA THOB PE
Venerated by the sons of the conqueror

།རྒྱལ་བའི་སྲས་ཀྱིས་ཤིན་ཏུ་བསྟེན་མ།

rgyal ba'i sras kyis shin tu bsten ma
JAL WE SE CHI SHIN TU TEN MA
Who have attained every single perfection.

།ཕྱག་འཚལ་ཏུཏྟཱ་ར་ཧཱུྃ་ཡི་གེ

phyag 'tshal tutta ra hung yi ge

(5) CHAG TSHAL TUT TA RA HUNG YI GE

Homage, Mother, filling all regions, sky, and the realm of desire

།འདོད་དང་ཕྱོགས་དང་ནམ་མཁའ་གང་མ།

'dod dang phyogs dang nam mkha' gang ma

DÖ DANG CHOG DANG NAM KHA GANG MA

With the sounds of TUTTARA and HUNG,

།འཇིག་རྟེན་བདུན་པོ་ཞབས་ཀྱིས་མནན་ཏེ།

'jig rten bdun po zhabs kyis mnan te

JIG TEN DÜN PO ZHAB CHI NEN TE

Trampling the seven worlds with her feet,

།ལུས་པ་མེད་པར་འགུགས་པར་ནུས་མ།

lus pa med par 'gugs par nus ma

LÜ PA ME PAR GUG PAR NÜ MA

Able to summon all before her.

།ཕྱག་འཚལ་བརྒྱ་བྱིན་མེ་ལྷ་ཚངས་པ།

phyag 'tshal brgya byin me lha tshangs pa
(6) CHAG TSHAL JA JIN ME LHA TSHANG PA
Homage, Mother, worshipped by Indra, Agni, Brahma,

།རླུང་ལྷ་སྣ་ཚོགས་དབང་ཕྱུག་མཆོད་མ།

rlung lha sna tshogs dbang phyug mchod ma
LUNG LHA NA TSHOG WANG CHUG CHÖ MA
By the Marut and different mighty ones.

།འབྱུང་པོ་རོ་ལངས་དྲི་ཟ་རྣམས་དང་།

'byung po ro langs dri za rnams dang
JUNG PO RO LANG DRI ZA NAM DANG
Honored by the hosts of spirits, of yakshas,

།གནོད་སྦྱིན་ཚོགས་ཀྱིས་མདུན་ནས་བསྟོད་མ།

gnod sbyin tshogs kyis mdun nas bstod ma
NÖ JIN TSHOG CHI DÜN NE TÖ MA
Of gandharvas and the walking dead.

།ཕྱག་འཚལ་ཏྲཊ་ཅེས་བྱ་དང་ཕཊ་ཀྱིས།

phyag 'tshal trat ces bya dang phat kyis
(7) CHAG TSHAL TRET CHE JA DANG PHET CHI
Homage, Mother, destroying the magical devices of outsiders

།ཕ་རོལ་འཕྲུལ་འཁོར་རབ་ཏུ་འཇོམས་མ།

pha rol 'phrul 'khor rab tu 'joms ma
PHA RÖL THRÜL KHOR RAB TU JOM MA
With the sounds of TRET and PHET,

།གཡས་བསྐུམ་གཡོན་བརྒྱང་ཞབས་ཀྱིས་མནན་ཏེ།

g.yas bskum g.yon brgyang zhabs kyis mnan te
YE KUM YÖN JANG ZHAB CHI NEN TE
Trampling with her right leg bent and the left extended,

།མི་འབར་འཁྲུག་པ་ཤིན་ཏུ་འབར་མ།

me 'bar 'khrug pa shin tu 'bar ma
ME BAR THRUG PA SHIN TU BAR MA
Ablaze with a raging wildfire.

།ཕྱག་འཚལ་ཏུ་རེ་འཇིགས་པ་ཆེན་མོ།

phyag 'tshal tu re 'jigs pa chen mo
(8) CHAG TSHAL TU RE JIG PA CHEN MO
Homage, TURE, terrible lady,

།བདུད་ཀྱི་དཔའ་བོ་རྣམ་པར་འཇོམས་མ།

bdud kyi dpa' bo rnam par 'joms ma
DÜ CHI PA WO NAM PAR JOM MA
Who annihilates the warriors of Mara,

།ཆུ་སྐྱེས་ཞལ་ནི་ཁྲོ་གཉེར་ལྡན་མཛད།

chu skyes zhal ni khro gnyer ldan mdzad
CHU CHE ZHAL NI THRO NYER DEN DZE
Slaying all enemies with a frown

།དགྲ་བོ་ཐམས་ཅད་མ་ལུས་གསོད་མ།

dgra bo thams cad ma lus gsod ma
DRA WO THAM CHE MA LÜ SÖ MA
Of wrath on her lotus face.

།ཕྱག་འཚལ་དཀོན་མཆོག་གསུམ་མཚོན་ཕྱག་རྒྱའི།

phyag 'tshal dkon mchog gsum mtshon phyag rgya'i
(9) CHAG TSHAL KÖN CHOG SUM TSHÖN CHAG JE
Homage, Mother, her hand adorns her heart

།སོར་མོས་ཐུགས་ཀར་རྣམ་པར་བརྒྱན་མ།

sor mos thugs kar rnam par brgyan ma
SOR MÖ THUG KAR NAM PAR JEN MA
In a mudra that symbolizes the Three Jewels.

།མ་ལུས་ཕྱོགས་ཀྱི་འཁོར་ལོ་བརྒྱན་པའི།

ma lus phyogs kyi 'khor lo brgyan pa'i
MA LÜ CHOG CHI KHOR LO JEN PE
Adorned with the universal wheel,

།རང་གི་འོད་ཀྱི་ཚོགས་རྣམས་འཁྲུགས་མ།

rang gi 'od kyi tshogs rnams 'khrugs ma
RANG GI Ö CHI TSHOG NAM THRUG MA
She radiates turbulent light.

།ཕྱག་འཚལ་རབ་ཏུ་དགའ་བ་བརྗིད་པའི།

phyag 'tshal rab tu dga' ba brjid pa'i
(10) CHAG TSHAL RAB TU GA WA JI PE
Homage, Joyful Mother, whose brilliant diadem

།དབུ་རྒྱན་འོད་ཀྱི་ཕྲེང་བ་སྤེལ་མ།

dbu rgyan 'od kyi phreng ba spel ma
UR JEN Ö CHI THRENG WA PEL MA
Spreads out garlands of light,

།བཞད་པ་རབ་བཞད་ཏུཏྟཱ་ར་ཡིས།

bzhad pa rab bzhad tutta ra yis
ZHE PA RAB ZHE TUT TA RA YI
Subjugating Mara and the world

།བདུད་དང་འཇིག་རྟེན་དབང་དུ་མཛད་མ།

bdud dang 'jig rten dbang du mdzad ma
DÜ DANG JIG TEN WANG DU DZE MA
With a mocking, laughing TUTTARA.

།ཕྱག་འཚལ་ས་གཞི་སྐྱོང་བའི་ཚོགས་རྣམས།

phyag 'tshal sa gzhi skyong ba'i tshogs rnams

(11) CHAG TSHAL SA ZHI CHONG WE TSHOG NAM

Homage, Mother, able to summon before her

།ཐམས་ཅད་འགུགས་པར་ནུས་པ་ཉིད་མ།

thams cad 'gugs par nus pa nyid ma

THAM CHE GUG PAR NÜ MA NYI MA

All the host of protectors of the earth.

།ཁྲོ་གཉེར་གཡོ་བའི་ཡི་གེ་ཧཱུྂ་གིས།

khro gnyer g.yo ba'i yi ge hung gis

THRO NYER YO WE YI GE HUNG GI

Moving her frowning brows, she saves

།ཕོངས་པ་ཐམས་ཅད་རྣམ་པར་སྒྲོལ་མ།

phongs pa thams cad rnam par sgrol ma

PHONG PA THAM CHE NAM PAR DRÖL MA

From all poverty by the sound of HUNG.

།ཕྱག་འཚལ་ཟླ་བའི་དུམ་བུ་དབུ་རྒྱན།

phyag 'tshal zla ba'i dum bu dbu rgyan

(12) CHAG TSHAL DA WE DUM BÜ UR JEN

Homage, Mother, whose diadem

།བརྒྱན་པ་ཐམས་ཅད་ཤིན་ཏུ་འབར་མ།

brgyan pa thams cad shin tu 'bar ma

JEN PA THAM CHE SHIN TU BAR MA

Is a crescent moon, blazing with all her ornaments,

རལ་པའི་ཁྲོད་ན་འོད་དཔག་མེད་ལས།

ral pa'i khrod na 'od dpag med las

RAL PE TRÖ NA Ö PAG ME LE

Ever shining with the brilliant light

།རྟག་པར་ཤིན་ཏུ་འོད་རབ་མཛད་མ།

rtag par shin tu 'od rab mdzad ma

TAG PAR SHIN TU Ö RAB DZE MA

Of Amitabha in her piled hair.

༄ཕྱག་འཚལ་བསྐལ་པ་ཐ་མའི་མེ་ལྟར།

phyag 'tshal bskal pa tha ma'i me ltar

(13) CHAG TSHAL KAL PA THA ME ME TAR

Homage, Mother, residing amidst the garland that blazes

༄འབར་བའི་ཕྲེང་བའི་དབུས་ན་གནས་མ།

'bar ba'i phreng ba'i dbus na gnas ma

BAR WE THRENG WE Ü NA NE MA

Like the fire at the end of the world era,

༄གཡས་བརྐྱང་གཡོན་བསྐུམ་ཀུན་ནས་བསྐོར་དགའི།

g.yas brkyang g.yon bskum kun nas bskor dga'i

YE CHANG YÖN KUM KÜN NE KOR GE

Right leg extended, left bent, encompassed by joy,

༄དགྲ་ཡི་དཔུང་ནི་རྣམ་པར་འཇོམས་མ།

dgra yi dpung ni rnam par 'joms ma

DRA YI PUNG NI NAM PAR JOM MA

Annihilating hosts of enemies.

།ཕྱག་འཚལ་ས་གཞིའི་ངོས་ལ་ཕྱག་གི།

phyag 'tshal sa gzhi'i ngos la phyag gi

(14) CHAG TSHAL SA ZHI NGÖ LA CHAG GI

Homage, Mother who hits the earth with the palm of her hand,

།མཐིལ་གྱིས་བསྣུན་ཅིང་ཞབས་ཀྱིས་བརྡུང་མ།

mthil gyis bsnun cing zhabs kyis brdung ma

THIL JI NÜN CHING ZHAB CHI DUNG MA

Who pounds on it with her feet,

།ཁྲོ་གཉེར་ཅན་མཛད་ཡི་གེ་ཧཱུྃ་གིས།

khro gnyer can mdzad yi ge hung gis

THRO NYER CHEN DZE YI GE HUNG GI

Frowning wrathfully, she shatters

།རིམ་པ་བདུན་པོ་རྣམས་ནི་འགེམས་མ།

rim pa bdun po rnams ni 'gems ma

RIM PA DÜN PO NAM NI GEM MA

The seven underworlds by the sound of HUNG.

།ཕྱག་འཚལ་བདེ་མ་དགེ་མ་ཞི་མ།

phyag 'tshal bde ma dge ma zhi ma
(15) CHAG TSHAL DE MA GE MA ZHI MA
Homage, Mother, blissful, virtuous, calm,

།མྱ་ངན་འདས་ཞི་སྤྱོད་ཡུལ་ཉིད་མ།

mya ngan 'das zhi spyod yul nyid ma
NYA NGEN DE ZHI CHÖ YÜL NYI MA
Whose field of activity is peaceful nirvana,

།སྭ་ཧ་ཨོཾ་དང་ཡང་དག་ལྡན་པས།

sva ha om dang yang dag ldan pas
SO HA OM DANG YANG DAG DEN PE
Endowed with the true perfection of SOHA and OM,

།སྡིག་པ་ཆེན་པོ་འཇོམས་པ་ཉིད་མ།

sdig pa chen po 'joms pa nyid ma
DIG PA CHEN PO JOM PA NYI MA
Destroying great evils.

།ཕྱག་འཚལ་ཀུན་ནས་བསྐོར་རབ་དགའ་བའི།

phyag 'tshal kun nas bskor rab dga' ba'i
(16) CHAG TSHAL KÜN NE KOR RAB GA WE
Homage, Mother, encompassed by joy,

དགྲ་ཡི་ལུས་ནི་རབ་ཏུ་འགེམ་མ།

dgra yi lus ni rab tu 'gem ma
DRA YI LÜ NI RAB TU GEM MA
Who shatters the bodies of enemies,

།ཡི་གེ་བཅུ་པའི་ངག་ནི་བཀོད་པའི།

yi ge bcu pa'i ngag ni bkod pa'i
YI GE CHU PE NGAG NI KÖ PE
Savioress manifesting from the rigpa of HUNG,

།རིག་པ་ཧཱུྃ་ལས་སྒྲོལ་མ་ཉིད་མ།

rig pa hung las sgrol ma nyid ma
RIG PA HUNG LE DRÖL MA NYI MA
Arraying the sounds of the ten-syllable mantra.

།ཕྱག་འཚལ་ཏུ་རེའི་ཞབས་ནི་བརྡབས་པས།

phyag 'tshal tu re'i zhabs ni brdabs pas

(17) CHAG TSHAL TU RE ZHAB NI DAB PE

Homage, TURE, stamping her feet,

།ཧཱུྃ་གི་རྣམ་པའི་ས་བོན་ཉིད་མ།

hung gi rnam pa'i sa bon nyid ma

HUNG GI NAM PE SA BÖN NYI MA

Whose seed appears in the form of HUNG,

།རི་རབ་མནྡཱ་ར་དང་འབིགས་བྱེད།

ri rab mnda' ra dang 'bigs byed

RI RAB MAN DA RA DANG BIG CHE

Shaking Mount Meru, Mandara, Binduchal,

།འཇིག་རྟེན་གསུམ་རྣམས་གཡོ་བ་ཉིད་མ།

'jig rten gsum rnams g.yo ba nyid ma

JIG TEN SUM NAM YO WA NYI MA

And the triple world.

།ཕྱག་འཚལ་ལྷ་ཡི་འཚོ་ཡི་རྣམ་པའི།

phyag 'tshal lha yi 'tsho yi rnam pa'i
(18) CHAG TSHAL LHA YI TSHO YI NAM PE
Homage, Mother holding the rabbit-marked moon,

།རི་དྭགས་རྟགས་ཅན་ཕྱག་ན་བསྣམས་མ།

ri dvags rtags can phyag na bsnams ma
RI DAG TAG CHEN CHAG NA NAM MA
Which is like a heavenly lake,

།ཏ་ར་གཉིས་བརྗོད་ཕཊ་ཀྱི་ཡི་གེས།

ta ra gnyis brjod phat kyi yi ges
TA RA NYI JÖ PHET CHI YI GE
Dispelling all poison with the sound of PHET

།དུག་རྣམས་མ་ལུས་པར་ནི་སེལ་མ།

dug rnams ma lus par ni sel ma
DUG NAM MA LÜ PAR NI SEL MA
And the twice-spoken TARA.

།ཕྱག་འཚལ་ལྷ་ཡི་ཚོགས་རྣམས་རྒྱལ་པོ།

phyag 'tshal lha yi tshogs rnams rgyal po
(19) CHAG TSHAL LHA YI TSHOG NAM JAL PO
Homage, Mother served by the ruler of the hosts of gods,

།ལྷ་དང་མི་འམ་ཅི་ཡིས་བསྟེན་མ།

lha dang mi'am ci yis bsten ma
LHA DANG MI AM CHI YI TEN MA
By the gods and kinnaras,

།ཀུན་ནས་གོ་ཆ་དགའ་བས་བརྗིད་ཀྱིས།

kun nas go cha dga' bas brjid kyis
KÜN NE GO CHA GA WE JI CHI
Dispelling conflicts and bad dreams

། རྩོད་དང་རྨི་ལམ་ངན་པ་སེལ་མ།

rtsod dang rmi lam ngan pa sel ma
TSÖ DANG MI LAM NGEN PA SEL MA
With her armor of joy and splendor.

།ཕྱག་འཚལ་ཉི་མ་ཟླ་བ་རྒྱས་པའི།

phyag 'tshal nyi ma zla ba rgyas pa'i
(20) CHAG TSHAL NYI MA DA WA JE PE
Homage, Mother, whose two eyes

སྤྱན་གཉིས་པོ་ལས་འོད་རབ་གསལ་མ།

spyan gnyis po las 'od rab gsal ma
CHEN NYI PO LE Ö RAB SAL MA
Are the sun and full moon, shining with brilliant light,

།ཧ་ར་གཉིས་བརྗོད་ཏུཏྟ་ར་ཡིས།

ha ra gnyis brjod tutta ra yis
HA RA NYI JÖ TUT TA RA YI
Who dispels deadly disease

།ཤིན་ཏུ་དྲག་པོའི་རིམས་ནད་སེལ་མ།

shin tu drag po'i rims nad sel ma
SHIN TU DRAG PÖ RIM NE SEL MA
With TUTTARA and twice-spoken HARA.

ཕྱག་འཚལ་དེ་ཉིད་གསུམ་རྣམས་བཀོད་པས།

phyag 'tshal de nyid gsum rnams bkod pas

(21) CHAG TSHAL DE NYI SUM NAM KÖ PE

Homage, Mother, endowed with the power to pacify

ཞི་བའི་མཐུ་དང་ཡང་དག་ལྡན་མ།

zhi ba'i mthu dang yang dag ldan ma

ZHI WE THU DANG YANG DAG DEN MA

By the array of the three natural states,

གདོན་དང་རོ་ལངས་གནོད་སྦྱིན་ཚོགས་རྣམས།

gdon dang ro langs gnod sbyin tshogs rnams

DÖN DANG RO LANG NÖ JIN TSHOG NAM

Destroying the hosts of evil spirits, yakshas, and the
walking dead,

འཇོམས་པ་ཏུ་རེ་རབ་མཆོག་ཉིད་མ།

'joms pa tu re rab mchog nyid ma

JOM PA TU RE RAB CHOG NYI MA

TURE, most excellent Mother.

༄༅། །རྩ་བའི་སྔགས་ཀྱི་བསྟོད་པ་འདི་དང་།

rtsa ba'i sngags kyi bstod pa 'di dang
TSA WAI NGAG CHI TÖ PA DI DANG
This is the praise with the root mantra,

།ཕྱག་འཚལ་བ་ནི་ཉི་ཤུ་རྩ་གཅིག།

phyag 'tshal ba ni nyi shu rtsa gcig
CHAG TSHAL WA NI NYI SHU TSA CHIG
And these are the twenty-one homages.

།ལྷ་མོ་ལ་གུས་ཡང་དག་ལྡན་པའི།

lha mo la gus yang dag ldan pa'i
LHA MO LA GÜ YANG DAG DEN PE
Reverently recited by whoever has intelligence

།བློ་ལྡན་གང་གིས་རབ་དད་བརྗོད་དེ།

blo ldan gang gis rab dad brjod de
LO DEN GANG GI RAB DE JÖ DE
And genuine devotion to the goddess,

ཿསྲོད་དང་ཐོ་རངས་ལངས་པར་བྱས་ནས༔

srod dang tho rangs langs par byas nas
SÖ DANG THO RANG LANG PAR JE NE
Arising at dawn or evening to remember it,

ཿདྲན་པས་མི་འཇིགས་ཐམས་ཅད་རབ་སྟེར༔

dran pas mi 'jigs thams cad rab ster
DREN PE MI JIG THAM CHE RAB TER
It grants complete fearlessness.

ཿསྡིག་པ་ཐམས་ཅད་རབ་ཏུ་ཞི་བྱེད༔

sdig pa thams cad rab tu zhi byed
DIG PA THAM CHE RAB TU ZHI JE
All evil deeds are pacified;

ཿངན་འགྲོ་ཐམས་ཅད་འཇོམས་པ་ཉིད་དོ༔

ngan 'gro thams cad 'joms pa nyid do
NGEN DRO THAM CHE JOM PA NYI DO
All evil destinies are destroyed.

།རྒྱལ་བ་བྱེ་བ་ཕྲག་བདུན་རྣམས་ཀྱིས།

rgyal ba bye ba phrag bdun rnams kyis

JAL WA JE WA THRAG DÜN NAM CHI

Quickly, one will be initiated

།མྱུར་དུ་དབང་ནི་བསྐུར་བར་འགྱུར་ལ།

myur du dbang ni bskur bar 'gyur la

NYUR DU WANG NI KUR WAR JUR LA

By the seventy million buddhas.

།འདི་ལས་ཆེ་བ་ཉིད་ནི་འཐོབ་ཅིང་།

'di las che ba nyid ni 'thob cing

DI LE CHE WA NYI NI THOB CHING

Attaining greatness by this practice,

།སངས་རྒྱས་གོ་འཕང་མཐར་ཐུག་དེར་འགྲོ།

sangs rgyas go 'phang mthar thug der 'gro

SANG JE GO PHANG THAR THUG DER DRO

One will proceed to the ultimate state, buddhahood.

ཌེ་ཡིས་དུག་ནི་དྲག་པོ་ཆེན་པོ།

de yis dug ni drag po chen po
DE YI DUG NI DRAG PO CHEN PO
Even if one has eaten or drunk

བརྟན་གནས་པའམ་གཞན་ཡང་འགྲོ་བ།

brtan gnas pa'm gzhan yang 'gro ba
TEN NE PA AM ZHEN YANG DRO WA
A dreadful poison, vegetable or animal,

ཟོས་པ་དང་ནི་འཐུང་པ་ཉིད་ཀྱང་།

zos pa dang ni 'thung pa nyid kyang
ZÖ PA DANG NI THUNG PA NYI CHANG
By remembering the praise, the poison is completely dispelled.

དྲན་པས་རབ་ཏུ་སེལ་བ་ཉིད་འཐོབ།

dran pas rab tu sel ba nyid 'thob
DREN PE RAB TU SEL WA NYI THOB
One completely abandons the hosts of sufferings

།གདོན་དང་རིམས་དང་དུག་གིས་གཟིར་བའི།

gdon dang rims dang dug gis gzir ba'i

DÖN DANG RIM DANG DUG GI ZIR WE

Caused by evil spirits,

།སྡུག་བསྔལ་ཚོགས་ནི་རྣམ་པར་སྤངས་ཏེ།

sdug bsngal tshogs ni rnam par spangs te

DUG NGAL TSHOG NI NAM PAR PANG TE

Contagious diseases and poisons,

།སེམས་ཅན་གཞན་པ་རྣམས་ལ་ཡང་ངོ་།

sems can gzhan pa rnams la yang ngo

SEM CHEN ZHEN PA NAM LA YANG NGO

For other beings as well.

།གཉིས་གསུམ་བདུན་དུ་མངོན་པར་བརྗོད་ན།

gnyis gsum bdun du mngon par brjod na

NYI SUM DÜN DU NGÖN PAR JÖ NA

If one recites the praise clearly two, three, or seven times,

ཁུ་འདོད་པས་ནི་བུ་ཐོབ་གྱུར་ཞིང༌།

bu 'dod pas ni bu thob gyur zhing
BU DÖ PE NI BU THOB JUR ZHING
Those wishing for sons will gain sons.

ཁོར་འདོད་པས་ནི་ནོར་རྣམས་ཉིད་ཐོབ།

nor 'dod pas ni nor rnams nyid thob,
NOR DÖ PE NI NOR NAM NYI THOB
Those wishing for wealth will gain wealth.

འདོད་པ་ཐམས་ཅད་ཐོབ་པར་འགྱུར་ལ།

'dod pa thams cad thob par 'gyur la
DÖ PA THAM CHE THOB PAR JUR LA
All desires will be fulfilled.

བགེགས་རྣམས་མེད་ཅིང་སོ་སོ་འཇོམས་འགྱུར།

bgegs rnams med cing so so 'joms 'gyur
GEG NAM ME CHING SO SO JOM JUR
There will be no hindrances, all obstacles will be destroyed.

APPENDIX

NAMES AND ATTRIBUTES

Name of Tara*	Her Color	Her Hand Object	Her Activity according to Outer Level
1. Nyurma Pamo	red	conch shell	swift, heroic liberation from sufferings
2. Loter Yangchenma	white	mirror	sound of peace, harmony, truth, and wisdom
3. Sönam Tobché	golden	wish-fulfilling jewel	increases merit and prosperity
4. Tsugtor Namgyalma	golden	nectar vase	increases life force and longevity
5. Wangdü Rigjé Lhamo	red	bow and arrow	magnetizes beneficial wisdom essences
6. Jigjé Chenmo	dark red	phurba/dagger	subdues invisible beings, mental disturbances
7. Zhengyi Mithubma	blue-black	flaming sword	destroys internal and external artifices
8. Zhengyi Migyalma	dark red	flaming vajra	destroys maras, subdues illusions
9. Sengdeng Nagchi	green	dharma wheel	protects from all outer and inner fears
10. Jigten Sumlé Gyalma	rich red	victory banner	subdues worldly distractions, arrogance

Name of Tara*	Her Color	Her Hand Object	Her Activity according to Outer Level
11. Phagma Norter Drölma	orange-red	treasure vase	gives wealth, removes sufferings of poverty
12. Tashi Dönjé	gold/yellow	infinite knot	inner and outer balance, timely seasons, harvests
13. Yüllé Gyalma	dark red	open vajra	stops warfare, enmity; heals destruction of anger
14. Thronyer Chen	blue/black	tung shing/pestle	crushes subtlest negativities and obstacles
15. Rabzhima	rich white	small vase	purifies greatest evils and obscurations
16. Rigngag Tobjom	red	double dorje	destroys bad intentions and their source, ego
17. Pagmé Nönma	orange	golden stupa	stops violent activites such as robbery, hunting
18. Maja Chenmo	white	rabbit-marked moon	protects against outer and inner poisons; protects infants and children
19. Dugkarmo	white	white umbrella	protects from nightmares, disputes, curses
20. Ritö Loma Jönma	saffron	za ma tog	dispels epidemics and deadly illness
21. Lhamo Özer Chenma	white	golden fish	protects life force, brings inner radiance; protects animals

* *Each name is prefixed by an honorific title, either Jetsün Drölma or Noble Lady Tara.*

References

Tibetan Sources and Sadhanas

The Blessing Treasure: A Liturgy of the Buddha (Thub chog byin rlabs gter mdzod bzhugs so). Sidney, N.Y.: Dharma Samudra, 1994.

H.H. Düdjom Rinpoche. *The Daily Recitation of Revered Noble Tara* (Rje btsun sgrol ma'i rgyun khyer ni). Sidney, N.Y.: Dharma Samudra, 1997.

Jigme Lingpa. *The Inner Practice of the Queen of Great Bliss* (Yum ka'i nang sgrub).

Jo Nang Taranatha. *The Origin of Tara Tantra* (Sgrol ma'i rgyud kyi byung khung gsal bar byed pa'i lo rgyus gser gyi phreng ba zhes bya ba). Translated and edited by David Templeman. Dharamsala: Library of Tibetan Works and Archives, 1981.

A Small Treasury of Prayers of Supplication and Dedication (Gsol 'debs dang bsngo smon nyung bsdus bzhugs so). Sidney, N.Y.: Dharma Samudra, 1996.

WESTERN TEACHINGS, SOURCES, AND TRANSLATIONS

Beer, Robert. 2003. *The Handbook of Tibetan Buddhist Symbols*. Boston: Shambhala.

Beyer, Stephan. 1978. *The Cult of Tara: Magic and Ritual in Tibet*. Berkeley: University of California Press.

Bokar Rinpoche. 1999. *Tara, the Feminine Divine*. San Francisco: ClearPoint Press.

Chodron, Thubten. 2005. *How to Free Your Mind: Tara the Liberator*. Ithaca: Snow Lion Publications.

Düdjom Rinpoche, Jigdral Yeshe Dorje. 1991. *The Nyingma School of Tibetan Buddhism: Its Fundamentals and History*. 2 vols. Trans. and ed. Gyurme Dorje and Matthew Kapstein. Boston: Wisdom Publications. [Abbreviated as NS in Endnotes]

Kangyur Rinpoche. 2001. *Treasury of Precious Qualities: Commentary on the Root Text of Jigme Lingpa entitled* The Quintessence of the Three Paths. Trans. the Padmakara Translation Group. Boston: Shambhala.

Kunzang, Eric Pema. 1999. *Rangjung Yeshe Dictionary*. Kathmandu: Rangjung Yeshe Translations and Publications. [Abbreviated as RYD in Endnotes]

Palden Sherab Rinpoche, Khenchen. 2004. *The Smile of Sun and Moon: A Commentary on the Praise to the Twenty-one Taras*. Trans. and ed. Anna Orlova. Boca Raton: Sky Dancer Press.

Willson, Martin. 1986. *In Praise of Tara*. Boston: Wisdom Publications.

ENDNOTES

[1] Palden Sherab Rinpoche 2004.

[2] The Third Turning of the Wheel of Dharma is the final group of Buddha Shakyamuni's teachings, including the sutras on the definitive meaning. The Buddha placed the emphasis on buddha-nature, the union of luminosity and emptiness devoid of constructs.

[3] Yeshe Tsogyal was a nirmanakaya emanation of Tara and Vajrayogini in the form of a Tibetan princess of the time of Guru Padmasambhava. From her earliest years she was completely committed to practicing Dharma. Rather than accepting a conventional path of marriage, she became Guru Rinpoche's consort and attained the highest realizations. Her power of memory was so profound that she was able to transcribe all of his teachings. These preserved teachings were hidden as termas for future generations. Yeshe Tsogyal attained the transcendental wisdom rainbow body .

[4] Guru Jobar (1172-1231) was born into the family of a heart student of Chetsün Senge Wangchuk. Until about age seven he appeared to be dumb, but then his wisdom blazed forth and he swiftly became highly realized.

[5] The term "Mother Tantra" as used in the New Schools is more or less synonymous with the term "Anuyoga" used in the Ancient tradition. It refers to completion stage practices that work with the inner channels, winds, and essences (or tsa, lung, and thigle).

[6] This development, called the *Rimé* [ris med] movement, saw the breaking down of the factionalism among the major schools with an outburst of renewed scholarship, practice, and realization.

[7] Jamyang Khyentse Wangpo (1820-1892) is renowned as the combined emanation of King Trisong Deutsen and Vimalamitra. He was born in Kham, and from his earliest youth displayed tremendous intelligence. He sought out and received ordination, vows, and empowerments from masters of every school, and fully trained himself in these practices. His enlightened activities were remarkable: in particular it is said that there was nothing which he did not teach at least once, fulfilling the hopes of every student.

[8] Jamgön Kongtrül Lodro Thaye (1813-1899) was an emanation of Ananda, Buddha Shakyamuni's cousin and devoted attendant, and the great translator Vairochana. He was a prodigious scholar, and is renowned today for the encyclopedic treatises [mdzod] he composed covering all the Tibetan arts and sciences. He became a great treasure revealer and protector in conjunction with Jamyang Khyentse Wangpo.

[9] Mipham Rinpoche (1846-1912), whose full name was Mipham Jamyang Namgyal Gyamtso, was born in Kham. He received extensive teachings from both Kongtrül and Khyentse and showed profound understanding of the difficult points of reasoning of the philosophical schools, as well as high attainment in the practice of Manjushri and the Great Perfection. He was noted at the time for composing treatises explaining the view and practices of the Old tradition, and defending them brilliantly in debate with scholars of the New Schools. Many of his writings have been translated into English, and are being studied and practiced by Western students.

[10] Tseringma is the foremost of the five Long-Life Deities. These were originally mountain-guardian spirits, and they plagued the great Tibetan yogi Milarepa during his cave retreats. They were tamed by Vajravarahi and converted to Buddhism: Tseringma became Mila's consort. She is usually shown as a white figure riding a snow lion and carrying a long-life vase in her right hand.

[11] Chögyur Dechen Lingpa (1829-1870), born in Kham, was an emanation of Yeshe Rolpatshal (a son of King Trisong Deutsen). He was a

great treasure revealer. "From each treasure site came forth an exceedingly large number of doctrines, sacramental substances, images and sacred objects."[NS] Most of his discoveries were made in the presence of large crowds of witnesses. He is the author of the beautiful prayer to Guru Padmasambhava which begins *Du Sum Sangye Guru Rinpoche*.

[12] Rongzom Chökyi Zangpo was born in the Tsang area of Tibet. With a quick and profound brilliance and infallible memory, he completed his philosophical studies by his thirteenth year. He received the teachings of Guru Padmasambhava, Vairochana, and Aro Yeshe Jungne. He acted as translator and interpreter for many of the Indian panditas of the New Translations, which were being completed in the eleventh century.

[13] It is from Taranatha's scholarly work *The Origin of Tara Tantra* that much of the detailed knowledge of the history and lineages of Tara practice is derived.

[14] The Jonang School emphasizes the Kalachakra Tantra. Its philosophical tenets are based on the *shentong* view of the Madhyamaka.

[15] Jigme Lingpa (1730-1798) was born in Pelri, as the combined emanation of Vimalamitra, King Trisong Deutsen, and Gyalse Lharje. He lived in a period when the teachings of the Ancient Translation School of the Nyingmapas had declined and become very sparse. As a result of his great learning and powerful realization, while in retreat Jigme Lingpa received the direct blessings of Longchenpa's body, speech, and mind. With this authorization he became the uniquely gifted source of the *Nyingthig*, or "Heart Essence," teachings of Dzogchen, which are increasing and spreading in our current times.

[16] Briefly, we use the term *relative truth* to designate phenomena perceived through the ordinary six senses, processed by the conceptual mind, and capable of being expressed in speech. We use the term *ultimate truth* to refer to a wisdom state that is beyond concepts and dualities and that is inexpressible.

[17] Very similar "guidance" was experienced by the young Machig Labdrön, who also refused to be drawn in by the conceptual dualistic biases of gender.

[18] Mount Potala is a pure land in the southern direction. An historical Mount Potala in South India is considered by Hindus to be the realm of Shiva, but by Buddhists to be the pure land of Avalokiteshvara and Tara. In Tibet, the Potala Palace is the residence of Avalokiteshvara's human emanations, the Dalai Lamas.

[19] The six realms of samsaric existence are the three lower realms (hell realm, hungry ghost realm, and animal realm) and the three upper realms (human realm, jealous god realm, and god realm). All of the innumerable beings within these realms, whether visible to human eyes or invisible to us, are subject to suffering. Thus the bodhisattva vows to save each and every one.

[20] It is said that sentient beings are numberless as the stars in the universe. Yet the bodhisattva courageously and heroically vows to save them all from suffering.

[21] The eight great fears are the fear of enemies, lions, elephants, fire, poisonous snakes, brigands, imprisonment, and floods.

[22] The Sanskrit term *tathagatagarbha* has many meanings, including buddha-nature, buddha-seed, and womb of buddhahood, all of which relate to the recognition of our ultimate Tara nature as that which gives rise to enlightenment.

[23] A buddha appears in the sambhogakaya, or enjoyment body emanation, to be perceived by and teach to bodhisattvas and very highly realized human masters. A buddha appears in a nirmanakaya, or emanation body form, because that can readily be perceived by the class of samsaric beings among which he or she intends to give teachings and relieve sufferings.

[24] Duality refers to the ignorant habit pattern of the unenlightened mind which deludedly interprets experience in terms of separate and

solid subject and objects, or self and others. As translated here, the word "duality" may refer to the dualistic appearance itself [gnyis snang], or to dualistic grasping [gnyis 'dzin], our ignorant habit of holding on to this error as the truth. Common examples of dualities are such paired concepts as right/wrong, unclean/clean, here/there, and high/low. The enlightened mind, on the other hand, realizes the ultimate truth of nonduality [gnyis med.]

[25] These various forms are known as *natsog tülku* [sna tshogs sprul sku].

[26] The Praise to the Twenty-one Taras is a section within the tantra *In Praise of Tara, The Mother of All Tathagatas*.

[27] The terms "basic level" or "basic Buddhism schools" are used to refer to what elsewhere may be called the Hinayana or Theravadin schools. The Rinpoches use these terms in order to stress that these teachings are basic to all aspects of Buddhist thought and practice.

[28] Ten bhumis [sa bcu] are the ten levels of a noble bodhisattva's development into a fully enlightened buddha. On each stage more subtle defilements are purified and a further degree of enlightened qualities is manifested. These ten are: the Joyous, the Stainless, the Radiant, the Brilliant, the Hard to Conquer, the Realized, the Reaching Far, the Unshakeable, the Good Intelligence, and the Cloud of Dharma.

[29] In relation to these various enumerations of twenty-one, Khenpo Tsewang Dongyal Rinpoche refers readers to the One Hundred Thousand Stanza Prajnaparamita text *Abhisamayalankara*, and to *Gateway to Knowledge*, a commentary on this text by Jamgön Mipham Rinpoche.

[30] Senge Dongma is a wisdom dakini in the Dzogchen tradition. She is dark blue-black, has a lion's face with semiwrathful expression, and holds the dakini's attributes, the skull cup and curved knife.

[31] Tröma Nagmo is primarily associated with the Chöd practice. She is a form of Vajravarahi, is black and extremely wrathful, and has a sow's head behind her ear.

32 The five primary wisdom dakini consorts of Guru Padmasambhava are: the Indian princess Mandarava; the Nepalese dakinis Kalasiddhi and Shakyadevi, with whom he practiced Yangdag Heruka and Vajrakilaya at Yanglesho; the Tibetan princess Yeshe Tsogyal; and the Bhutanese dakini in tiger form, Mönmo Tashi Kyedren, with whom he practiced as Dorje Drolö. The Tiger's Nest hermitage was named after her.

33 The third eye is one of the specific marks of a dakini. According to Simmer-Brown, this is one of a series of marks specific to dakinis that are found in Vajrayana teachings: these compare with the major and minor marks of a buddha found in the sutra teachings.

34 Clairvoyance or "omniscient all-seeing" [thams cad gzigs pa nyid] is described as a state in which all beings and all phenomena of all times in all directions can be perceived simultaneously without any one phenomenon blocking any other.

35 Tantra is "the Vajrayana teachings given by the Buddha in his sambhogakaya form. The real sense of tantra is 'continuity,' the innate buddha-nature, which is known as the 'tantra of the expressed meaning.' The general sense of tantra is the extraordinary tantric scriptures also known as the 'tantra of the expressing words.' Tantra may also refer to all the resultant teachings of Vajrayana as a whole." [RYD]

36 The term "vase body" is a Dzogchen term for buddha-nature.

37 Khenpo Tsewang Dongyal Rinpoche gives this illustration of the relationship between the literal and the symbolic meanings.

The literal verse says,

> The sun is shining
> The crows are cawing,
> The farmers are plowing,
> The robbers are crying.

The symbolic meanings are,

> The Buddha has come into the world,
> The students are chanting and practicing,
> The patrons are performing meritorious activities,
> The forces of negativity are driven away.

[38] The Buddha Samantabhadra is the primordial dharmakaya buddha. His consort is Buddha Samantabhadri. Tara is a nirmanakaya aspect of Samantabhadri's primordial wisdom nature.

[39] Of the Dhyani Buddhas, who are also the buddhas of the five directions, Buddha Vairochana is in the center, Buddha Vajrasattva is in the east, Buddha Ratnasambhava is in the south, Buddha Amitabha is in the west, and Buddha Amoghasiddhi is in the north.

[40] The five wisdoms are aspects of how the cognitive quality of buddha-nature functions. They are the dharmadhatu wisdom, mirror-like wisdom, wisdom of equality, discriminating wisdom, and all-accomplishing wisdom. Each is associated with one of the five Dhyani Buddhas.

[41] The Tibetan name for this pure land, *'og min*, means "beneath none." In other words, it is the highest of enlightened realms, the pure realm of the dharmakaya.

[42] According to the Vajrayana classification, tantric teachings are divided into two major categories, outer tantra and inner tantra. There are three outer and three inner tantras. The three outer tantras are named the Kriyatantra, Upayatantra, and Yogatantra. The three inner tantras in the Nyingma School are the Mahayogatantra, Anuyogatantra, and Atiyogatantra. The essence of all six categories of tantra is skillful means (love and compassion) and wisdom.

[43] The lunar month is divided into two halves, waxing and waning. Thus there are two tenth days—the waxing tenth day and the waning tenth day. The second day after the full moon is the first waning

day. Thus, the twenty-fifth day of the lunar month will be the waning tenth day.

44 There are special mantras for each of the twenty-one emanations of Tara, which may be found in Palden Sherab Rinpoche 2004.

45 The *dam pa sum* [dam pa gsum] may also be translated as "three holy ones," "three excellences," "three sacred aspects," or "three frames."

46 The "Prayer of the Four Immeasurables" invokes for all beings boundless love, compassion, joy, and equanimity.

47 As used in Palden Sherab Rinpoche 2004.

48 This is the abhaya mudra in Sanskrit or *mi 'jigs pa'i phyag rgya* in Tibetan.

49 This is the varada mudra in Sanskrit or *mchog sbyin gyi phyag rgya* in Tibetan. Tara holds this mudra downwards to symbolize her activity of subjugating the object of fear.

50 Palden Sherab Rinpoche 2004 contains additional details on the hidden meanings.

51 Trekchö [khregs gcod] is "cutting through the stream of delusion, the thoughts of the three times, by revealing naked awareness devoid of dualistic fixation. To recognize this view through the oral instructions of one's master and to sustain it uninterruptedly throughout all aspects of life is the very essence of Dzogchen practice." [RYD] Trekchö emphasizes ka dak, or the view of primordial purity.

52 The term "vajra" in this context should be understood as designating an indestructible reality.

53 The left leg is drawn in to symbolize Tara's self-discipline and the right leg is extended to symbolize her readiness to swiftly rise to help beings.

54 The right-turning conch shell, one of the eight auspicious sym-

bols, signifies the fearless proclamation of the truth, or the Dharma.

[55] A Small Treasury of Prayers of Supplication and Dedication (söl deb dang ngo mön nyung du zhug so).

[56] Longchen Rabjampa (1308-1363) was one of the greatest masters of the Nyingma School. He was a brilliant scholar, highly realized master, and a prolific and penetrating writer. He had a deep relationship with the dakinis, who assisted his activities throughout his life.

[57] Tsongkhapa (1357-1419) was the founder of the Gelugpa School, a master of philosophy, and a prolific writer of commentary, analysis, and poetry. He had profound devotion to Tara.

[58] The mirror is the symbol of emptiness and pure consciousness. It is impartial and unaffected by what it reflects, revealing all phenomena to be empty in essence.

[59] The Tibetan term *rigpa* is used in two ways, which may lead to misunderstanding if one is not aware of the context. Here in the teaching on the general meaning, it is used in the sense of "conceptual knowledge or understanding." In the ultimate meaning teachings, rigpa is used in its Dzogchen sense of "innate intrinsic awareness," which is nonconceptual wisdom.

[60] The white element, or white thigle, is received from the father at conception. It is associated with the cool lunar energy.

[61] Jigme Lingpa's *Yönten Dzö* [Yon ten mdzod], with his autocommentary, *Shingta Nyamnyi* [Shing rta mnyam gnyis], is often expounded as a summary in the curriculum of scholarly studies in the Nyingma schools.

[62] Paramita, or *pha röl tu phyin pa* in Tibetan, literally means "crossing over" or "reaching the other shore." In Mahayana usage it means perfecting an enlightened quality and transcending concepts of subject, object, and action.

[63] Tummo practice is the first endeavor in the Six Yogas. It enables the practitioner to generate intense physical heat. Mastery is often demonstrated by the ability to cause damp cloths draped over the shoulders to dry.

[64] Indra, while a very powerful deity, was himself also within samsara and, thus, his powers were not up to the job.

[65] This stupa is called the *phag pa shing kun chö rten* and it contains a self-born crystal stupa. The image of the stupa occasionally self-projects onto the night sky, where it has been seen by thousands of people as recently as the summer of 2005.

[66] As his practice had been prolonging his life, he chose to reverse its effect by chanting it in reverse.

[67] The long-life vase, or *tse bum*, is held by all the deities associated with long life, including Amitayus, White Tara, and Ushnishtavijaya. Guru Padmasambhava holds a long-life vase in his skull-cup.

[68] The red element is obtained from the mother at conception and it is associated with the hot solar energies.

[69] Tögal [thod rgal] is to jump over, "to skip grades," or cross in one leap. It is the highest Dzogchen practice, which emphasizes spontaneous presence [lhun grub].

[70] The concluding sound of this syllable falls to Western ears between an "M" and an "NG" sound. Thus readers will encounter both HUM and HUNG in various books. The transliteration HUNG has been chosen here.

[71] Kurukulle's bow and arrow are often represented as made of flowers, symbolizing the combined danger and attraction of the objects of the senses. In this iconographic tradition, which derives from Longchenpa, the bow and arrow are unadorned.

[72] Palden Sherab Rinpoche 2004, p. 59.

[73] Ibid., p. 63.

[74] The phurba, or ritual dagger, is a tantric implement associated with Vajrakilaya and other wrathful deities. Its symbolic use is for the subjugation of powerful negative forces, demons, and obstacles.

[75] There are different ways of indicating this Sanskrit syllable in the Roman alphabet. We have chosen to use PHET. It is pronounced as P'e, with a vowel intermediate between "ay" and "eh" and an extremely short, cut-off sound of "t."

[76] The wisdom sword [ye shes ral gri] can cut through ignorance. As the implement of wrathful deities, it severs and destroys demons and enemies of realization.

[77] The wrathful vajra is made of meteoritic iron. Oftentimes its points are open and sparking, although not in the image used here. It symbolizes Tara's vajra wrath.

[78] The dharmachakra symbolizes the Dharma's power for swift spiritual transformation, as well as the Buddha's three great teachings, known as the three turnings of the wheel.

[79] This is another of the eight auspicious symbols; in ancient times these adorned the chariots and processions of victorious kings. The victory banner became a Buddhist emblem to symbolize Buddha Shakyamuni's victory over the four maras.

[80] The ten directions are the four compass directions (north, east, south, and west), the four intermediate directions (northeast, southeast, southwest, and northwest), plus the directions of up and down.

[81] The treasure vase, called *ter ji bum pa* in Tibetan, is the attribute of wealth deities such as Phagma Norter Drölma. It overflows with inexhaustible jewels. Treasure vases are often placed or buried at key sites as offerings to the earth protectors and to promote peace and abundance.

[82] *Dgongs pa zang thal las kun bzang smon lam.*

[83] The endless knot, or glorious knot, [dpal be'u] is a very ancient symbol, dating back to at least 2500 B.C.E. in the Indus Valley. As a symbol of the Buddha's mind, it invokes continuity, love, and harmony. As it relates to the teachings, it symbolizes the twelve links of interdependent origination.

[84] See note 70. A similar phonetic rendering approach has been used.

[85] Usually the prongs of a vajra in the hand of a peaceful deity are rounded and closed, but in this case its prongs are standing straight and open. This symbolizes Tara's vajra wrath, which can destroy all negativities and even stop wars.

[86] Its symbolism is the concentration or crushing of various experiences and subtle negativities into "one taste."

[87] In Tibetan, [blo gros brtan pa].

[88] Vasubandhu was a great Indian master of the fourth century C.E., famed for writing the *Abhidharmakosha*, a treatise forming the basis of much of the philosophy of the basic Buddhism schools. Later in life he became convinced of the correctness of the Mahayana path and wrote major Yogacharin commentaries.

[89] SOHA is a workable way of reproducing the Tibetan pronunciation of the Sanskrit SVAHA.

[90] The vase and its anointing nectar symbolize the activity of purification. They wash away all mental obscurations and negative karma.

[91] *The Blessing Treasure: A Liturgy of the Buddha.*

[92] The double vajra is the emblem of Buddha Amoghasiddhi, the lord of the Karma family and the Dhyani Buddha of the northern direction, who in tantric sadhanas appears with Tara as his consort. It represents the all-accomplishing wisdom.

⁹³Palden Sherab Rinpoche 2004, p. 192, note 43.

⁹⁴ Rinpoche is referring humorously to the small mountain in the Catskills on which his monastery and retreat center are located.

⁹⁵ The stupa, or *chörten*, as a hand object represents the enlightened mind of the Buddha.

⁹⁶ Nagarjuna, a great Indian master of the first-second centuries C.E., is honored as the first human teacher of the Mahayana tradition of Madhyamaka, or the Middle Way.

⁹⁷ In Tibetan *ri wung* means "rabbit" and *ri dag* means "herbivore," an animal that eats only grass. So both rabbits and deer are included in the term *ri dag*. One of the Jataka tales recounting Buddha Shakyamuni's previous lifetimes tells that he was a compassionate hare that sacrificed his life to save others. The legend is that in honor of this, Indra placed the image of a rabbit upon the moon.

⁹⁸ Palden Sherab Rinpoche 2004, p. 144.

⁹⁹ She is named Sitatapatri in Sanskrit. As an individual deity practiced separately from the assembly of Taras, she is portrayed with one thousand arms, feet, and heads, and is completely covered with a billion eyes.

¹⁰⁰ The white umbrella symbolizes that she is held in the highest respect.

¹⁰¹ Epidemic sickness, both of humans and domestic animals, has always been one of the most feared processes in India and Tibet. The ability of the sun's light to dispel contagion is honored in all medical systems.

¹⁰² Palden Sherab Rinpoche 2004, p. 158.

¹⁰³ While a pair of golden fishes are among the eight auspicious symbols, a single golden fish symbolizes great realization and the ability to liberate beings from samsara. When Naropa first encountered his teacher, the mahasiddha Tilopa, he was cooking live fish on hot coals

and Naropa questioned him about this very "un-Buddhist" activity. Tilopa snapped his fingers and the fish came immediately back to life. The master explained that, while it looked to Naropa's unrealized vision like he was killing the fish, he was actually liberating them from samsaric existence.

[104] A bardo is an intermediate state of experience. There are generally said to be six bardos, three of which are associated with this life and three with the transition from one life to another.

[105] The Tibetan verse is:
> *na tog na na sang je* [sna rtogs na sna sangs rgyas]
> *nub tog na nub sang je* [nub rtogs na nub sangs rgyas]

or
> If morning realized, then morning buddhahood;
> If evening realized, then evening buddhahood.

[106] *Lo den* [blo ldan], meaning the wise person; the bodhisattva or one who has developed or aspires to develop bodhichitta.

p18 White Tara — tear from Chenrezig's left eye
     Green Tara — tear from Chenrezig's right eye
p23 Explanation of Tara's appearance in thangka
p232 Eight Great Fears (Perils)
p25 Significance of 21

Daka, dakini → khandro, khandroma (Tibetan)
                "sky walker"

dakini — "the activity of love and compassion,
          full of strength, moving freely in the
          wisdom space"
p27 Great emptiness, the mother of all the Buddhas
    "Emptiness is freedom; emptiness is great opportunity
     It is pervasive and all phenomena arise from it."
p29 Rainbow as metaphor for emptiness
    Hope, fear, and all our different emotions and
    experiences arise from futilely grasping at
    rainbows.

p33 Tantra → gyü (Tibetan) — "continuity, continuum"
    3 aspects of Tantra

    Ground (zhi)   Path (lam)   Fruit (dre bu)
         ↓   ↓   ↘
    True nature,   method & wisdom   meeting of moth
    tathagatagarbha,   ↓   and child
    "youthful vase body" nonattachment

                   ↓
              skillful means
                   ↓
              love and compassion

    Creation stage — skillful means to develop love
                     and compassion

    Completion stage — direct practice on nongrasping,
                       pass beyond relying on
                       conceptual imagination

p36 6 limits for understanding Tantra
   mundane or nonmundane meaning
   ordinary or hidden meaning
   literal or symbolic meaning

   4 systems — wording meaning
                general meaning
                hidden meaning
                ultimate meaning

40 pure land of Akanishtha, the pervasive land
which is beyond size and measure, the perfect
place beyond duality and cannot be understood
by dualistic thoughts
Vajrayana — timeless, uninterrupted teaching
The Buddha is giving these teachings now
in Akanishtha

41 Our meditation, practice, confidence,
commitment, and bodhicitta are the true shrine.

42 Setting up shrine

43 Earth's 24 power spots
            32 holy places
             8 great cemeteries

25th day of lunar month best for Tara practice